God
Sex
And
Your
Child

For additional information about John Nieder's speaking schedule, cassette tapes, or nationally syndicated radio program, "The Art of Family Living," write to:

The Art of Family Living
P.O. Box 2000
Dallas, Texas 75221

John Nieder

God Sex And Your Child

THOMAS NELSON PUBLISHERS
Nashville

Published in Nashville, Tennessee, by Thomas Nelson, Inc., and distributed in Canada by Lawson Falle, Ltd., Cambridge, Ontario.

Printed in the United States of America.

Scripture quotations are from the Holy Bible, New International Version. Copyright © 1973, 1978, 1984 International Bible Society. Used by permission of Zondervan Bible Publishers. Scripture quotations marked (ICB) are from the International Children's Bible, New Century Version. Copyright © 1986, Sweet Publishing.

Library of Congress Cataloging-in-Publication Data

Nieder, John.
   God, sex, & your child / John Nieder.
      p.   cm.
   Bibliography: p.
   ISBN 0-8407-7633-0
   1. Sex instruction—United States. 2. Sex instruction—Religious aspects—Christianity. 3. Sex in the Bible. I. Title. II. Title: God, sex, and your child.
HQ57.N54   1988
306.7'07—dc19
                                       88-25514
                                         CIP

Acknowledgments

My deepest appreciation to:

J. T. and Katie—for being the best kids a dad could ever have.

Howard Hendricks—for opening wide the door of ministry.

Trevor Mabery—for leaving me with a legacy of love.

John Trent and Gary Smalley—for blessing me with their friendship and encouragement.

Jon Campbell—for modeling commitment and dedication.

Al Sanders—for looking at me with eyes of faith.

Bill and Polly Croslin—for teaching me the priority of prayer.

Bill Barnard—for freeing me up to write.

Joy and Carlton Kupp—for counting us as friends and for Joy's gracious spirit while she typed and retyped the manuscript.

Bill Watkins at Thomas Nelson—for helping me to cut my writing teeth and for making vast improvements in this book.

Our listeners across the country—for sharing their hearts.

To Teri
Love, now and forever

Contents

Foreword

If you have ever wanted to walk beside a caring minister and take his professional pulse as he encounters hurting people who question and seek counsel, John Nieder allows such a privilege. He walks his readers into the ugly realities of our libertine age and uncovers the camouflage of crude indecency.

To talk about seduction and abuse can easily boil down to glorified sensationalism, unless, of course, we come to such carnality with solid rational solutions. In our world one can easily conclude that there is no hope for our children's chastity, that intimacy with virtue is part of history only. That lie is the deception of our spiritual enemy.

Problems of unrestraint are enormous, the dangers of debauchery are real, and the casualties are mounting. But the wanton ways of our world do not have to gain mastery over our children. Parents are the front-lines of defense. Nor are we the first generation in history to face such a hailstorm of harlotry. God has spoken on the subject of sex, and teaching His counsel on it to our children is part of getting back on the right track.

In her classic discussion on toddlerhood, Professor Selma Fraiberg of the University of California Medical School states that sexual satisfaction in adult life may be condensed in this statement:

Fulfillment in adult sexual experience depends upon the degree to which a man has confidence and pleasure in his masculinity and a woman has satisfaction and pleasure in her femininity and the degree to which both a man and a woman have given up their childhood attachments to parents and possess the means of loving completely a person of the opposite sex (*The Magic Years*, p. 210).

This echo of the essence of biblical teaching reminds us that our world cannot love adequately because we are buying the delusion that sexual encounters exist primarily for self-gratification instead of for pleasure and procreation within a lifelong marital commitment. We want to get instead of give.

John Nieder is a father of young children as well as a servant of Christ. Seldom have I had a student so ardently devoted to his calling, willing to face squarely the boobytraps laid for his own and other youngsters, to gently but firmly unhinge society's triggers, to expose its bait as cruel trickery. His platform has been the sound waves of radio and the adult Sunday school classroom. Now his voice penetrates the printed page. His call to relearn and reteach moral how-to's needs to be heard. His red flag waves over one of today's most critical needs.

HOWARD G. HENDRICKS
Distinguished Professor
Chairman of the Center for Christian Leadership
Dallas Theological Seminary
Dallas, Texas

Introduction

We have got to say something and we know it. We're uncomfortable, but we know that's not a good excuse.

So we decide to say something, but what do we say? How do we say it?

This book is about that something called sex which we must discuss with our children. With teen pregnancy at an all-time high and AIDS quickly becoming the price tag for promiscuity and perversion, we can no longer hesitate.

But what do we say? Let's say what God says. We can use the Bible to explain that sex is God's good gift designed for marriage.

In the following pages I will develop a scriptural strategy of protection and preparation. We will examine various ways we can safeguard our children from the devastation of sexual sin. Then we will discuss practical ways to prepare our children to walk the path of purity.

I can almost see it now. You and your child and an open Bible. The entire scene is wrapped in profound intimacy. Something sacred is taking place as your hearts are knit together by eternal truth.

May our Lord bless your efforts to etch His Word on the hearts and minds of your children.

John Nieder
Dallas, Texas

God
Sex
And
Your
Child

CHAPTER 1

Speak Now or the Wrong Person Will

"**J**ohn, I–I–I need to talk to . . . to you."

Her voice was so faint and strained that I barely recognized it. "Beth, is that you?" I asked, somewhat embarrassed.

A weak "yes" not only confirmed her identity—it revealed her broken heart. I asked her to come to my office the next morning, and she agreed.

After I hung up the phone, I reminisced about the Beth I once knew. She was a sweet, energetic high school girl who had earned straight A's and still found time to be a leader in our church youth group. With long brown hair and a magnetic smile, Beth was popular with young and old alike. And along with her gentle spirit and simple attire, Beth was also respected. Out of her strong commitment to Jesus Christ she had introduced her own mother to the Savior. But our brief telephone conversation made me seriously wonder if my memories of her would be rudely updated.

The following morning yielded the answer. When Beth entered the hallway leading to my office, her energy and innocence were gone. Confusion, shame, and despair marked not only her appearance but her every step. She seemed to want to run and hide; yet, somehow, she kept moving in my direction.

Halfway down the hall, she stopped and looked behind her. As if on a signal, a young man stepped out from around the corner. Tim, a lanky seventeen-year-old, was wearing jeans, a T-shirt, and Nike sneakers. His head was down, his shoulders slumped, and every step he took was a chore. His reluctance matched Beth's, so much so that it seemed the day would pass before they reached my door.

I wanted to make them feel comfortable. They obviously needed a friend. I introduced myself to Tim, who responded with downcast eyes and little more than a grunt.

Beth wanted to be the one to tell me why they had come, but her first words brought on a flood of tears. Within moments she was crying uncontrollably. I tried to reassure her: "Beth, it's going to be all right."

Suddenly, anger burst through her tears, and she screamed, "It's not all right—I'm pregnant!"

Motioning to Tim, I asked if Beth and I could talk alone for a few minutes. Once he left the room, Beth told me what had happened. She had met Tim several months before at a party following their high school football game. She didn't know if he was a Christian, so she invited him to church. He came several times, and they started to see each other regularly.

After a few weeks he began to pressure her sexually. When she resisted, he attempted to manipulate her with one line after another. Repeatedly he told her, "If you really loved me, you'd show it." When she refused to give in because of her beliefs, he followed up with, "Why not? Everybody else is doing it."

One night he asked her why she thought God didn't want them to have sex before they got married. After all, he reasoned, if they loved each other, God would certainly approve of their expressing their love physically. She didn't know what to say, but she still managed to refuse his advances.

Then one evening he gave her the typical ultimatum: "Either you go to bed with me tonight, or it's over between us!" With her emotions driving her desires for an intimate relationship, she surrendered her virginity. But rather than producing an emotional oneness, her surrender brought a sex-dominated relationship filled with secret rendezvous and deception. Their passions burned out of control, reducing their love to the mere fulfillment of physical pleasure and creating what they had dreaded most—a pregnancy.

IN THE WAKE OF THE SEXUAL REVOLUTION

Today's fast-moving current of sexual immorality has destroyed innumerable young lives. Many young people like Beth and Tim have been caught in its wake. Consider the facts.

Perverse sexual lifestyles once taboo and talked about only in private now receive public acceptance and support. Sexual immorality has led to the spread of numerous diseases that rage like forest fires out of control. The most feared of these diseases—AIDS—is so deadly it can ravage anyone who ventures even once into the arena of promiscuous sex. A study of some 160 thousand teenagers evidences how far our society has fallen from a Christian ethic.

One-third of teens between ages thirteen and fifteen have already engaged in sexual intercourse. Sixty percent of sixteen- to eighteen-year-olds have experienced intercourse. The average age for the first sexual encounter is between fifteen and seventeen. Although 90 percent of the students surveyed said they "believed" in marriage, 74 percent said they would live with someone prior to or instead of marriage.[1]

You would hope that the sexual behavior of *Christian* teens would follow a significantly different trend. But that's not the case. A recent study of teenagers in evangelical churches revealed that:

- by eighteen years of age, 43 percent have had sexual intercourse
- 39 percent see fondling breasts as sometimes morally acceptable
- 32 percent see fondling genitals as sometimes morally acceptable
- 65 percent of eighteen-year-olds have had some kind of sexual contact, from fondling breasts to intercourse
- 35 percent could not state that premarital sexual intercourse is always morally unacceptable.[2]

When a majority of teens have had some form of sexual contact by age eighteen, they are evidently learning about sex from someone. But from whom?

WHO WILL TEACH YOUR CHILD?

In my Sunday school class of some five hundred adults, fewer than a third indicated their parents had taught them about sex. When I asked the other two-thirds to remain after class for additional instruction, they laughed. Although their parents hadn't given them the facts, they were well versed in human sexuality.

The results of my informal survey were similar to those of a formal study of young people who attend Bible-believing churches. Only 23 percent of the youth surveyed received the bulk of their sexual knowledge from their parents, while 38 percent received it from their friends, just 13 percent from the Bible, and 7 percent from their local churches.[3]

Our children will learn about sex. The question is—from whom? If they don't learn about it from us, they will certainly be "educated" by their peers, the media, or their schools.

Their Peers

You probably got your first lesson on sex from a childhood friend. Do you recall where you were? How did you feel? Did you tell your parents? I happened to be in the backyard of my friend's house. I felt uneasy and betrayed by my parents as I heard about this unusual, secretive act. I didn't tell them about this experience because, like most kids, I wasn't sure how they would respond.

Consider your own experience with peers as your sexual instructors; then weigh the consequences of a neighborhood friend or classmate telling *your* child the "facts of life." How do you think your child would respond? What would the potential damage be, especially if you didn't discover what was conveyed? Perhaps I can help you make the calculations.

A neighborhood friend could rip open the curtain of sexual mystery long before your child can emotionally and intellectually deal with the information. In a matter of moments, your child's sweet innocence could be peeled away. One mother shared with me her daughter's response to the neighborhood "sexpert":

Our daughter, Wendy, was five years old and had been playing outside with an older neighborhood friend. I looked up from my ironing board as Wendy suddenly came running into the house, obviously distraught, crying, and saying, "It isn't so, is it? Tell me it's not true!" The little friend had been telling her the facts of how babies are made. At this time I was pregnant with our third child, and

Wendy had been happily engrossed in planning for the baby's arrival. She poured out the story; her little heart was horrified to think that it could possibly be true. It was too awful for her consideration.

Wendy's parents immediately and openly discussed what she had heard, thus minimizing the damage. But keep in mind, many children never tell their parents. Upset, confused, and embarrassed, they keep the misinformation locked up inside their minds, dwelling on it, picturing what they can.

Sharing secrets bonds children to their friends rather than to their parents. When two people share intimate information, bonding takes place. When bonding occurs, the pressure to conform intensifies. The writer of Proverbs expressed this truth when he warned his son not to be enticed by sinners. For sinners will say, "Throw in your lot with us, and we will share a common purse" (Prov. 1:14). In effect, our child's peers say, "Listen to us, and we will share a common secret"—a secret that unites them with their peers and may alienate them from their parents.

Years ago my wife and I witnessed firsthand how a secret can become as bonding as glue, even between siblings. After seeing ads for beer and wine, our children, then ages four and six, asked why we didn't have alcohol in our house. We explained some of our reasons, and that was the end of the conversation. Months later we found our children giggling uncontrollably. When we asked them why, they broke out laughing. My son marched triumphantly into the pantry and pulled out a bottle of nonalcoholic wine. They were in their glory thinking they had discovered our secret. It took me about an hour to explain that *non* meant no. It was then I discovered that a temporary solution to sibling rivalry is a sibling secret. As long as they shared a secret, they got along beautifully.

Unfortunately, ill-informed secrets about sex also glue our children to their friends—a bond that could push us out of a very important part of their lives.

The clandestine input of peers also heightens a child's interest in sex. When I was a junior in high school, a friend of mine and I dated two girls who happened to be friends. On Friday nights we would go to one girl's house to watch television together in the game room downstairs. Usually we would pair off and sit on separate couches. My date and I held hands and watched television and assumed that the other couple was doing the same.

One night as my friend and I left, he told me what he and his date were really doing while my date and I watched television. Just a few feet away from where we sat they were partially undressed and "petting." As he spoke I felt backward and ignorant. And yet his words intensified my interest and desires.

What happened to me isn't unusual. More than likely, one of your child's friends will feed him with information and images that will arouse his sexual appetite. The parents of a twelve-year-old boy who attended a Christian school told me of pressures from another boy in their son's school. They inadvertently overheard a phone conversation their son had with his classmate. They sensed their son was uncomfortable, so when he hung up, they asked him what was wrong. Eventually, he admitted that his "friend" was badgering him to explain why he hadn't had sex with his girlfriend. His Christian friend was making him feel guilty that he hadn't violated his virginity or that of an innocent Christian girl.

If you think Christian schools are a haven for your children, think again. The moral fabric of our kids is being ripped apart by our morally abusive society. Even Christian schools can't ward off the assault.

Peers will give a distorted view of sex. Children tend to assume that the information they receive reflects reality. Uninformed and naturally naive, they cannot accurately evaluate what their friends or classmates might say.

An eight-year-old boy was taken into custody by the local police after he molested a seven-year-old neighbor. This little boy admitted he fondled the girl but could not understand why he was in trouble. During questioning, the police officer found out that the boy, his older sister, mother, and father regularly had sex together. As far as this boy knew, family sex was normal.

How would you like this boy to tell your son or daughter about sex? If you don't educate your child, someone as confused as this eight-year-old just might.

Sexual distortion reigns supreme in our day, not only among misinformed children but also in the misdirected media.

The Media

In the 1950's, when Lucille Ball on *I Love Lucy* was expecting a child, the word *pregnant* was not allowed on the air. In the sixties, Rob and Laura on *The Dick Van Dyke Show,* though married, slept in twin beds. In the seventies, the female star on *I Dream of Jeannie* couldn't wear an outfit that would expose her navel.

How times have changed! Today's leading ladies wear so little that they can scarcely cover their navels. Sexually-laden terms and phrases are commonplace. And unmarried couples regularly share satin sheets strategically draped around their nude bodies so that practically nothing is left to the viewer's imagination.

This deluge of explicit sexual content in the media doesn't just reflect our society's change in values. It also greatly contributes to the shaping of *our* values and our children's. Impressionable young minds are daily titillated by the sexual messages pouring out of the television, videos, movies, and today's rock music. As educator Neil Postman points out, our children are being taught by the media, especially by television, and they're getting a course of study that fails to benefit their intellect or their character: "I think it accurate to call television a curriculum. As I understand the word, a curriculum is a specially constructed information system whose purpose is to influence, teach, train or cultivate the mind and character of youth. Television, of course, does exactly that, and does it relentlessly. In so doing, it competes successfully with the school curriculum. By which I mean, it damn near obliterates it."[4]

The subtle messages of television *are* relentless, and their over-sexed content reveals their perversity.

Not long ago, during a late-night study effort, I searched for a rebroadcast of the news. As I turned the dial, my tired eyes noticed something on a semiscrambled television screen. Looking more closely, I saw a totally unclothed couple engaged in oral sex. This was not cable television! The show came from a local station that partially scrambled its signal in order to sell its smut with a special decoder. I fought my desire to watch and turned the TV off, wondering how many teenagers (not to mention their parents) were up late watching X-rated sex on a scrambled screen.

Despite the rapid moral deterioration of television, it still runs a second to many videos and movies. Horrible sexually explicit and violent scenes in slasher films have a ready teen audience who watch them at "gross out" parties. One of the most popular films shows a woman taking a bath. It cuts away from a shot of her naked upper body to a man holding a nailgun just outside the bathroom door. With seductive radio music playing in the background, the man opens the door and shoots a nail into her forehead. Is that the kind of "entertainment" you want your child to watch?

Imagine your child staying at a friend's house and viewing the popular video *Friday the 13th,* with its close-up of the severed nude torso of a young lover resting in a pool of blood. Or picture her watching *I Spit on Your Grave,* in which a man bleeds to death from castration and several women fall victim to graphically portrayed gang rapes. Movies like these are readily accessible in video stores, where kids can rent almost any movie without regard to its rating.

As if all this weren't enough, the visual media has a strong ally in much contemporary rock music. In her disturbing book *Raising PG Kids in an X-rated Society,* Tipper Gore exposes the immorality that countless teens and preteens see at many rock concerts:

> [These rock concerts] are promoted by local radio stations which give away tickets and backstage passes. Thousands of parents ferry their youngsters—some nine, ten, and eleven years of age—to concert arenas, often with no idea what these children may hear or see there: profanities, details of sexual encounters, descriptions of the thrills of drinking and taking dope. The messages are all the more powerful because they come from stars whom many kids worship. Since outrageous showmanship substitutes for musical talent for many of these idolized groups, our concert-going children may well see performances involving simulated sexual acts or extreme violence.[5]

Perhaps you don't allow your child to attend rock concerts like those Gore describes, but what about MTV or other rock video shows?

One way or another, the media is teaching your child about sex.

Ironically and quite tragically, the media's message is also being reinforced in our schools.

The Public Schools

In response to the AIDS epidemic, Surgeon General C. Everett Koop has called for explicit sex education in schools, with information on homosexual as well as heterosexual relationships. More and more people support the idea that public schools should take the lead in teaching our children about sex. This possibility presents serious concerns for Christian parents who hold to a biblical ethic. Why? Because the schools will teach them a secular value system.

Public schools are teaching "safe sex" rather than abstinence. And they are claiming to do so in a value-free atmosphere! The guidelines below were handed out in a health class in a public high school in Austin, Texas. As you read them, think of your child being given these in class or hearing about them from a neighborhood friend who attends public school.

Safer Sex Guidelines for Women

If you are sexually active, unless you are in a mutually monogamous sexual relationship you are at risk of contracting and/or passing on sexually transmitted diseases (STDs), including AIDS. It is *your* responsibility to protect yourself.

1. Limit the number of your sexual partners.
2. Avoid exchanging body fluids, especially semen and blood. The virus has been isolated in saliva, but no known cases of AIDS have resulted from french or wet kissing only.
3. Use condoms for all vaginal, oral, and anal intercourse. Use condoms even if he seems like a real nice guy. STDs, including AIDS, don't discriminate. They can attack anyone, and you will not necessarily be able to tell if he's safe or not. He may not know, either, if he's safe or not.
4. Here are some tips for effective condom use:
   - roll the condom onto an *erect* penis
   - while rolling it on leave some room in the tip, so when he ejaculates ("comes"), it will have some place to go
   - for the same reason, make sure to squeeze the air out of the tip
   - after he ejaculates, hold onto the condom at the base of the penis while he withdraws the penis from your vagina, anus, or mouth

- *don't* use with vaseline; use water-based lubricants only
5. Feel shy about asking someone to use a condom? Maybe some of these will help:
   - Make it a rule, not an option . . . . "Do you want to put on the condom or shall I?". . .
   - You're at risk of exposure from those previous partners, too.
   - If you won't do it for yourself, do it to protect your future partners. . . .
     - Make it as fun as you can. Use colored condoms, or textured ones.
     - Make it erotic!
6. Don't forget there are a whole lot of other sensual, sexual activities you can do that are safe and fun. You can spend many long hours in these activities:
   - massage
   - masturbate each other
   - creative cuddling
   - pay attention to the entire body, not just the "usual" parts
   - mutual masturbation
   - take a bath together
   - hugging
   - long, lingering caresses
   - use your imagination

All STDs can be prevented. Not all can be cured.[6]

In the name of safe sex, high school students are told to use condoms for vaginal, anal, or oral intercourse. Teenage girls are reassured that suggesting a condom won't offend a partner—in fact, he will probably respect them all the more because of their interest in health! Unselfishness is extolled with the statement, "If you won't do it for yourself, do it to protect your future partners." Note the plural—partners. Monogamous relationships aren't even encouraged. Instead, immorality is promoted under the guise of safe, fun sex. Is this what educators mean by *value-free* education?

Public schools are also presenting deviant sexual practices as normal and acceptable. In a family life and health course taught in an Illinois high school, questions about the homosexual lifestyle are answered in an analogy with being right-handed or left-handed.

Then, in a student health book section titled "Family Health," the caption under a picture of two men embracing reads, "Research shows that homosexuals can lead lives that are as full and healthy as those of heterosexuals." This ninth-grade health book gives the rationale behind this "objective" viewpoint:

1. A person's biological sex results from a combination of genetic and hormonal influences that operate before birth. One's gender identity develops as a result of social and cultural conditioning that begins at birth.
2. The so-called sexual revolution is better termed the gender revolution. Today both men and women are more free to do and be whatever feels comfortable for them.
3. There are many options of sexual behavior: masturbation, petting, cunnilingus, fellatio, and intercourse. Other partner preferences besides heterosexuality include homosexuality and bisexuality.[7]

If this is value-free education, I'd like to see what value-laden education is like! Homosexuality and bisexuality are equated with monogamous heterosexual relationships. One lifestyle is taught to be no better or worse than another; all options are available and equally natural, healthy, and good. Is it any wonder that this type of education has led to a generation of young people who are sexually confused and abused?

A broken-hearted mother wrote to us at *The Art of Family Living* for prayer and counsel. Her beautiful seventeen-year-old daughter had just moved out because Mom and Dad had stumbled onto her lesbian lifestyle. Her mother told us that her daughter's school never discouraged homosexuality. Indeed, it made light of homosexuality's sinfulness by putting on a comical play about it during her daughter's senior year.

With the school system giving such positive exposure to homosexual practices, an increasing number of confused teens have wrongly assumed, along with this poor girl, that their immoral sexual explorations are normal and acceptable.

As public schools employ this secular approach to sex educa-

tion, they heighten the peer pressure on children who want to avoid premarital sex. By promoting "safe sex," the schools implicitly condone premarital sex. Even by referring to young people as sexually active, the schools project a positive image of an illicit life-style. After all, who wants to be known as being sexually passive?

Some years ago, a dedicated Christian girl told me of an experience at a local high school. While straightening up her locker, she found herself surrounded by five classmates. One by one they asked her to confirm the rumor that she was really a virgin. Although intimidated, she admitted her virginity, only to receive the ridicule of her classmates as a reward. She stood there alone—against peers who had embraced a value system our public schools have openly endorsed.

Our children can learn about sex from the media, their friends, and the schools. But the best place for a child to learn about sex is in the home with Mom and Dad as the teachers. To give our children anything less may rob them of a healthy, biblical view of their sexuality.

The noise of our day cannot drown out the quiet voice of God that whispers to the hearts and minds of parent and child alike. When we listen to Him, we have hope and a plan for victory. A plan that requires moms and dads to provide spiritual and sexual guidance for their children. A plan I will develop in the pages that follow.

GIVE IT SOME THOUGHT

1. Which of your child's friends would be most likely to communicate sexual information?

2. Does your child have a favorite TV program? If so, what does it teach your child about sex? Look for subtle as well as obvious messages.

3. Has your child gone to a movie recently? If so, what was it about? How was it rated? Was the rating for language, violence, or sexually explicit scenes?

4. What does the school teach your child about sex? Have you examined the course your child will be taught?

5. What opportunities have you had to teach your child a biblical view of sex? What opportunities might you have in the days ahead?

6. What kind of model does your child see in you and in others living at home?

7. What does your child know about sex? Is his understanding scripturally based?

CHAPTER 2

You *Can* Teach Your Child

Talking about sex with our children isn't easy, no matter what Masters and Johnson and Dr. Ruth have to say. Our inner turmoil frequently causes us to approach sex education in several misguided and, at times, humorous ways.

Some parents take the *creative* approach. Mom or Dad asks questions and tells stories, but neither ever mentions the word *sex*. "Son, have you ever wondered why there are so many birds in the sky? So many bees in the trees? So many giraffes in the zoo?" In the creative approach parents produce a *National Geographic* special but never get to the bottom line.

Another parental sex education curriculum involves the *crisis* approach. The crisis occurs when a child asks a difficult or unexpected question about sex. Take, for example, an eleven-year-old girl asking her mom, "How many times a week do you and Dad have sex?" At that moment the mother has a crisis! This mother was prepared, however. She kept her composure on the outside and told her daughter, "Go ask your father. He keeps count."

Another approach parents often use is the *confrontational* approach. They give their child the biological basics, then threaten to kill him if he decides to apply them.

Do any of these approaches look familiar? I guess I have used every one at sometime or other. Although some of our more feeble attempts deserve a good laugh, it's time we dedicated ourselves to teaching our kids what God says about sex.

OBSTACLES TO OVERCOME

But following God's approach to sex education is not always easy. In fact, you may need to clear some hurdles before you can really influence your children to adopt God's plan for their sexuality. One of these obstacles is embarrassment.

The Birds and the Bees and My Shaking Knees

"But John," you may say, "you just don't understand. I get all tongue-tied and break out in a cold sweat even at the thought of discussing sex with my child. The last time the topic came up I was a candidate for CPR! Can't I just give him a nice book and have him read the facts for himself?"

Making light of parental inhibitions concerning sex, Candyce H. Stapen has suggested various ways children can open the lines of communication with their parents. She tells kids:

- Parents are often embarrassed about sex, and have a few of their own hang-ups. . . .
- Recognize your values may differ. . . .Kids do not need to have the same values as their parents, but kids need to recognize their parents' values.[1]

How does that grab you? Someone is trying to tell your child how to talk to *you* about sex so *you* won't blush. And by the way, she wants your child to know you may have some sexual hang-ups as well as different values—values your children need not accept. Do you want someone with views like these teaching your child about sex? If not, then you need to get over your embarrassment, and that requires discovering its causes. Let's consider some of the more common ones.

In the inner chambers of our minds, some of us do not fully accept lovemaking in marriage as a good gift from God. It remains a taboo largely because of negative perceptions forced on us by the silence or misguided attitudes of our own parents. One woman wrote me: "My mother started by giving a moral view of sex, but not really a biblical one. She was and still is a nominal Christian, but then she shared various times with me how much she hated sex, describing the details with me. I also heard her talking to my aunt different times, wishing she could cut his 'thing' off. I spent many years lustfully looking at guys and sort of fantasizing, knowing that I wanted to enjoy it, not hate it like my mother did."

Grown children from homes that had a more balanced perspective may still find it difficult to discuss sex openly. For example, a young woman who grew up in a Christian home where she learned the value of personal purity got married and four years later became pregnant with her first child. Her husband was filled with excitement. He suggested that they call her parents and tell them the good news. But she said no. Perplexed, her husband asked why. With her emotional sensitivity heightened by the changes in her body, she was so reluctant that she suddenly blurted out, "Because they will know we *do* it!" After the initial shock, he tried to assure her that after four years of marriage, her parents probably would not be surprised.

Another reason we are reluctant to discuss biblical sexuality with our children is a sense of being out of step with the world. *The growing disparity between God's view of sex and our society's makes us feel uneasy.*

One afternoon after a racquetball game, I experienced the anxiety that comes when your values run against the current of those around you. In the locker room several men started discussing their sexual conquests. Although they didn't know me, they made several casual gestures to include me in their conversation. When I ignored them, dark clouds of alienation fell over the room like a Los Angeles smog. Feeling judged by my silence, they made me an outcast.

With indiscriminate sex raining down on our minds and the minds of our children, we can slowly begin to doubt our biblical value system. When those doubts grow, we sometimes wave the white flag and surrender to our more promiscuous culture.

The road to victory over embarrassment begins when we start to reprogram our minds with God's Word. Our inhibitions will disappear once we fully appreciate that our God is not the least bit ashamed to discuss sex. Keep in mind the following facts:

- God created sex and defines the parameters for its enjoyment.
- God gave us His plan and purpose for sex before sin entered human experience.
- The Word of God straightforwardly discusses various sexual problems and practices such as incest, rape, homosexuality, bestiality, adultery, venereal disease, and prostitution.
- The Song of Solomon and many other passages describe the joy of sex within the marital union.

Since the Author of our sexuality does not hesitate to discuss sex, neither should we. We should never be afraid to discuss what God was not afraid to create.

But the hard fact is that too many of us are shaking in our boots and keeping our mouths shut in a day when we can't afford to be timid. For this very reason, Surgeon General C. Everett Koop has called for explicit sex education in schools, even down to the elementary school level. The threat of AIDS must be dealt with, but as the Surgeon General laments, "Most parents are so embarrassed and reluctant [to talk about sex to their kids], you can't count on [their] getting the message across at home."[2] What an indictment! If we can't be relied on to educate our children about sex in the face of this deadly epidemic, when can our kids, much less our society, count on us to offer a helping hand? Are we going to allow our discomfort to put our children in life-threatening situations . . . to force our public officials to initiate a sex education program that ignores and undermines a Christian ethic? God forbid! We dare not hide in a corner hoping that everything will somehow work out. We must clearly and convincingly inform our kids of God's view of sex. If we don't, our kids will pay dearly for our silence.

The Pain from the Past

During the research phase of this book, I asked listeners from *The Art of Family Living* radio broadcast to share with me some of their experiences. After carefully reading numerous letters, I noticed how many parents felt inadequate to discuss the biblical view of sexuality because of their own personal failure to follow God's divine directives. This excerpt from one young mother's letter is typical: "I became a Christian when I was 23 years old and had already become involved with sex before my conversion. My thoughts, feelings and ideas on the subject were very much colored by my experience and I had to make a diligent effort to learn the correct way to teach my children about sex. I had no idea how to go about teaching my children and I felt my immorality prior to my conversion really messed me up on the subject."

Sexual sin has a way of haunting us. When we least expect it, the memories assault our minds and emotions, causing us to classify ourselves as worthless failures. Furthermore, the past can distort our present perspective on sex, leading us to seriously question our ability to teach our children the unadulterated truth. The question lingers: Can someone who failed teach someone else to succeed? No matter how hard we try, we seem unable to fend off the invasion of past pain. But it doesn't have to remain this way if we decide to learn from our past rather than linger in it. We *can* choose to use the past to impair our efforts or improve them. Our kids can benefit from our pain or be plagued by it. The choice lies in our willingness to deal with the past God's way.

If this hurdle is looming before you, let me suggest a series of steps you can take to put it behind you and experience the freedom you need to talk to your child. You probably already know the first step: *Ask God to forgive you and believe that He has*. Cling to the promise of 1 John 1:9: "If we confess our sins, he is faithful and just and will forgive us our sins and purify us from all unrighteousness." Notice, the verse doesn't say He *might* forgive us. It says He *will*. The only condition is our asking Him to forgive us. We, including you, can count on Him to do the rest.

Second, while standing on His promised forgiveness, *commit yourself to a life of personal purity*. When Jesus forgave a woman caught in adultery, He told her, "Go now and leave your life of sin" (John 8:11). Once God wipes *your* slate clean, take Jesus' advice—strive to keep it clean.

Divinely forgiven and recommitted, take the third step: *Forgive yourself*. Colossians 3:13 says, "Bear with each other and forgive whatever grievances you may have against one another. Forgive as the Lord forgave you." Although the passage directly applies to forgiving others, its principle indirectly applies to self-forgiveness.

You can and must forgive yourself. But doing so is often one of the hardest steps anyone can take.

"But how?" you ask. Start to view yourself as God views you. As far as He is concerned, your past sin is over and done with—not only forgiven but forgotten. He is not like so many of us, a score-keeper and recorder of wrongs. Though He is grieved and angered by our sin, He doesn't hold it against us if we take it before Him and seek His forgiveness. As the psalmist revealed so many centuries ago:

> The LORD is compassionate and gracious,
>   slow to anger, abounding in love.
> He will not always accuse,
>   nor will he harbor his anger forever;
> he does not treat us as our sins deserve
>   nor repay us according to our iniquities.
> For as high as the heavens are above the earth,
>   so great is his love for those who fear him;
> as far as the east is from the west,
>   so far has He removed our transgressions from us.
>   (Ps. 103:8–12)

Of course, you can really believe this and still have a difficult time forgiving yourself. The problem, however, lies with your feelings toward your past, not with God's view of it. Sexual sin generates strong emotions that are hard but not impossible to dispel. Once you realize this, you can begin to rid yourself of emotional baggage by turning it over to God each time it attempts to weigh you down. He can handle it, and He wants to. As the apostle Peter expressed it, "Cast all your anxiety on him because he cares for you" (1 Pet. 5:7). Simply say, "Lord, I know You have forgiven me of my sin, so I turn over to You my lingering sense of guilt." Your guilt feelings may not disappear over night, but if you continue to lay them at the foot of God's throne, they eventually will.

Now consider a fourth step in dealing with past failures: *Forget the past and press on for the prize* (Phil. 3:13). Forget means we put it out of our mind and don't allow it to drain our emotions. The only time we allow ourselves to remember is to learn objectively from the experience. We have all fallen in this race called life. God does not care how many times we have already fallen. All that matters to Him—and all that should matter to us—is how we will run the race that remains. We can either pout about the past or press on toward the future. God says, "Press on!" Why? To gain the prize. What prize? His praise for the way we run the race in the days we have left to live for Him.

One final step is needed to secure the freedom of forgiveness: *Look for the good that God can bring from your past*. One evening two of my friends and I discussed the difficult pressures our children face growing up today. All of us shared that we didn't want our children to flounder in the moral garbage we did before becoming Christians. Thinking about our talk later, I realized that the Lord has used our past indiscretions to enhance our sensitivity to our children's battles. Our failures can be the bricks that pave the way for our children's success.

So ask God to forgive you; commit to personal purity; forgive yourself; press on; and allow your past to help you build your child's future. Believe me, you'll be glad you did.

I Don't Know How

While embarrassment and regrets plague a significant number of Christian parents, even more feel inadequate to talk about sex because they lack the requisite knowledge. I don't mean biological facts about sex. If you're a parent, you obviously have at least a rudimentary understanding of these. But simply knowing how to make love does not mean you know what the Bible says about it or how to teach the biblical perspective to your child. Do you feel you know how to respond biblically to your child's questions about sex? Do you have a conscious, systematic plan to teach your children what God says on this subject? Since you're reading this book, I gather you're at least interested, if not committed, to the process and want to know. Well, let's start at the beginning.

Where does teaching begin? It begins with the teacher's knowledge of the topic. A friend of mine often says, "You cannot impart what you do not possess." But that poses a problem. Many Christians are biblically illiterate. So they need to grow beyond Bible babyhood on this topic. If they don't, they'll run into the problems this couple described in a letter to me:

Please speak to parents, like ourselves, who have raised their children in a mainline Protestant denomination only to discover that we, as well as our children, were "Bible babies" even though we've been to church nearly every Sunday since they've been born. We became aware of this deficiency about the time our oldest daughter left for college, and we only had one year to "coach" our youngest daughter before she left for college. My husband and I became very active in Bible Study Fellowship, and we now put Bible study into action and application in our daily lives. We share biblical insights with our children when the opportunity presents itself, and, of course, we pray for them daily.

We did end up changing denominations with our children's blessing and are in a class with other parents who have had a similar experience. As you know, there are parents who do not remove their families from churches which are not teaching the Bible or supporting Bible study. When these parents become aware of their deficiency, they are going to need some guidance about how to introduce biblical concepts about sex for various ages of children. And the older the child, the more frightened the parents, because of what they didn't say to that child when he was at a more accepting age, especially now that AIDS is a threat to our entire society.

I have written this book for you, the Christian parent. It doesn't matter whether you're a Bible babe or a knowledgeable Bible student. As long as you want to know how to communicate divine principles to your child on the most intimate and beautiful act any man and woman can enjoy, you have the right book. Let's not delay any longer. Let's jump in at the heart of the subject: the unique opportunity and responsibility you have to teach your child God's view of sex.

YOU ARE YOUR CHILD'S BEST TEACHER

My heart sank when I failed to make the all-star team after my final year of little league baseball. When I was asked to play on a back-up team, I only felt worse. My father sensed my disappointment and offered to help me work on my swing. Reluctantly, I agreed. We spent an afternoon practicing at a neighborhood field.

A couple of days later our back-up team played against the all-stars. When I came up to bat this time, I had a sense of confidence.

I stood there perfectly positioned, took a deep breath, and drilled the very first pitch over the center-field fence for a home run. I couldn't believe it! In four years of league playing, I had never hit a home run. Yet the first three times at bat, I cleared the fence—and on one of those occasions, I even hit a grand slam. (Incidentally, on my fourth time at bat I got over-confident and struck out!)

How did a frustrated alternate become a Babe Ruth overnight? It happened because someone close to me took the time to teach me the fundamentals. My dad taught me what to do and how to do it. Then he convinced me I *could* do it. That was all I needed.

As Christian parents, we have a divine commission to teach and challenge our children to live for Jesus Christ. No one else has been given that authority, responsibility, or privilege. God has designed them to look to us for instruction. When we fail to meet their need, we run the risk of programming them for failure in the Christian life. Part of the instruction they need revolves around their God-given sexuality. The Bible reveals several reasons why we should play the primary and predominant role in teaching our kids about sex.

You Are a Link in the Chain of Truth

An ancient command of the Jewish faith echoes its message across time to twentieth-century Christian parents: "These commandments that I give you today are to be upon your hearts. Impress them on your children. . ." (Deut. 6:6–7). For generations the golden chain of truth has been linked by parents who taught their children God's principles for living. And their families have been divinely blessed as a result.

Grandmother Lois and Mother Eunice built spiritual realities into the life of Timothy. Despite having to contend with an unbelieving spouse, Eunice teamed up with her mother to teach Timothy the sacred writings. Then, when the apostle Paul needed an assistant, he chose young Timothy who had a sterling reputation in the city of Lystra.

Most of us know full well that we should guide our children in God's way. But the thought of doing so frequently brings to the surface deep-seated guilt and a profound sense of inadequacy. We hear whispered in our ears, "You can't do it. . . . You don't know the Bible well enough. . . . You don't know what to say."

Don't listen! You *can* teach your child God's view of sex. You *can* teach your son or daughter how to maintain sexual purity and why doing so is crucial to their well-being. What God commands can be done, because He *never* calls us to a task without supplying everything we need to accomplish it. But our first step must be choosing to obey Him.

You Can Maximize Teachable Moments

The home is the laboratory in which a child defines and explores life. Even when an unborn baby brother or sister is inside Mom, lessons about life and love are being learned by those who are awaiting the arrival.

When our second child was born, my son, then just two years old, suffered from a severe case of sibling rivalry. One day he gave it to me straight: "Dad, I not like baby—let's take back to hospital." Fortunately, I took advantage of this choice moment to teach my son several important truths. I told him that both he and his sister were special gifts from God and examples of how much Mom and Dad love each other.

I must admit that after I shared all these wonderful ideas with my son, he still wanted to return his sister to the hospital. I can understand his feelings. Some days I have wanted to take both of them back! But at least the foundation was laid for him to see his sister and himself as special gifts from God.

These teaching opportunities do not just occur in your child's younger years. Your teen daughter may have an unmarried, pregnant friend. She can help illustrate several lessons that may prevent your daughter from making the same mistake. A commercial for condoms can open more advanced discussions about sex with teenage sons or daughters.

You Can Model the Message

Children are notorious for doing what we do rather than what we say. That's why modeling our message is absolutely essential. If we want our children to enjoy sex according to God's plan, we need to let them see mutual respect and love between Mom and Dad.

The Bible stresses the importance of modeling. Jesus Christ said to his disciples, "As I have loved you, so you must love one another" (John 13:34). The apostle Paul encouraged the Corinthians: "Follow my example as I follow the example of Christ" (1 Cor. 11:1).

What kind of in-house example are you to your child? Does she see Mom and Dad discreetly embracing? Or does she see them bracing for another battle? Remember, children learn far more from what they see than from what they hear.

When I first started preaching, a number of people told me I sounded like Dr. Howard Hendricks. They were right and I knew why. In the early years of our radio ministry, Dr. Hendricks was the teacher, and I did everything else, including editing his tapes. After listening to him for hundreds of hours, I literally could not help imitating some of his gestures and expressions.

Even today my gifted friend's imprint remains heavy. But as one person pointed out—I couldn't find a better model for communication.

What happened to me happens to our children. They virtually absorb our patterns and practice, which gives us a staggering potential impact.

You Have the Advantage of Age and Experience

Getting older does not guarantee that we get wiser, but age does give us the opportunity to learn from our experiences, good or bad. Looking back over my life, I realize I have learned a number of lessons the hard way. Now as a dad I hope to turn my past failures into my children's successes. They need not pay the price I paid. Granted, they may decide to ignore the wisdom I've gained and go their own ways, but at least I can offer them a chance to avoid some of the potholes of my past.

Throughout Proverbs we read a father's advice to his son. Calling upon his wisdom and experience, the father describes the allure of a prostitute and then warns his son:

My son, pay attention to my wisdom, listen well to my words of
  insight,
that you may maintain discretion and your lips may preserve
  knowledge.
For the lips of an adulteress drip honey, and her speech is
  smoother than oil;
but in the end she is bitter as gall, sharp as a double-edged
  sword.   (Prov. 5:1–4)

Just think of the heartache you may save your child as you follow
the model of the wise writer of Proverbs.

You Can Communicate Your Love

When we love someone unconditionally, we pave the way for true
intimacy. Unconditional love operates at a time of failure or transparency. When we fail and someone still loves us—it is unconditional and it is intimate. When we open ourselves up and expose our
insecurity and someone still loves us, that love is unconditional and
intimate.

Reassuring your son that wet dreams and spontaneous erections
are perfectly normal . . . explaining your daughter's menstrual cycle and reassuring her that it's normal . . . telling your son or
daughter who is soon to be married how to enjoy their marital union to the fullest, all these communicate acceptance and build
intimacy—intimacy that can last a lifetime—between you and your
child.

God has placed you in a position no one else can occupy in the
life of your child. And because of your relationship you can teach
your child a biblical view of sex better than anyone else. You can
and you must. In the chapters that follow you'll see how.

GIVE IT SOME THOUGHT

1. How would you describe your present approach to educating your child
about sex?

2. What are the obstacles you will need to overcome in order to teach your
child a biblical view of his or her sexuality?

3. What steps can you take to eliminate the embarrassment often associated with discussing sex with your child?

4. What kind of model are you providing for your child?

5. Are you willing to accept your God-given responsibility to teach your child a biblical view of sex?

CHAPTER 3

The Rape of Innocence

Everyone knew him as an innocent young boy, who lived with his parents in the Bay area of San Francisco. That's why no one could believe the accusations. And yet it turned out to be true. This boy, just twelve years old, had performed oral sodomy on a four-year-old neighborhood girl.

On a talk show, his attorney described his young client not as a criminal but as a victim. Weeks before this boy molested the girl, another boy had given him a dial-a-porn phone number while at church. With the number safely hidden away, he went into the pastor's vacant office and placed the call. Over the days that followed, he called the number (and others he was given) dozens of times, each time being exposed to messages describing perverted sexual acts in explicit detail. With so many erotic images in his head, he finally acted them out on an unsuspecting little girl.

In the case of this young boy the correlation between exposure and behavior was obvious. Before he heard the messages, the thought of oral sodomy never would have entered his mind. Instead, the information challenged his naturally immature conscience.

Each day, through countless avenues, children are exposed to information they can't handle emotionally, morally, or spiritually. Bombarded by sex-saturated messages, they become curious beyond their comprehension. Then some of the seeds of sexual interest germinate in an act of perversion or promiscuity that may change their lives permanently.

The exploitation of children is just one of the horrible tragedies of the "sexual revolution." A growing number of children are being sexually abused, often at the hands of someone whose passions have been fueled by pornography. But an even greater number of our kids are also being violated when they are exposed to explicit sexual material that overwhelms their moral defenses.

MORAL ABUSE

I call this attack *moral abuse* because it is an assault on the innocent and the vulnerable. Insidious and destructive, it blinds its victims through overexposure while it rapes them of their innocence.

Moral abuse is the violation of a child's innocence which occurs when a child is exposed to sexual information he cannot comprehend or that overwhelms his moral defenses.

Our society no longer safeguards the emotional and spiritual lives of our children. Instead, they have become victims of the mass marketing of sex. They are pawns to be manipulated for the personal pleasure of perverts and profiteers.

Children are bombarded with explicit sexual messages years before they have any need to know about the intricacies of physical union. Adolescents and teens who can comprehend normal sexual intercourse now must deal with sodomy, transvestites, AIDS, and bestiality. In addition, they are seduced by provocative messages that take advantage of their raging hormones.

Why is moral abuse a danger for our children? For several very important reasons.

The onslaught of explicit messages comes long before our children have developed the emotional and spiritual capacity to judge the information correctly. Even in the teen years they have yet to develop the emotional and spiritual insight to discern the dangers of immoral lifestyles which are flaunted on the evening news and presented as acceptable alternatives to monogamous heterosexuality.

Older children face another form of moral abuse that has shattered the lives of thousands of our youth. While their sexual desires are at a peak, everywhere they turn sensual messages scream for their attention and toy with their desires. A commercial for Guess jeans shows a teenage boy carrying a girl to the back seat of a car. The next shot is of the girl disheveled, with her blouse open, suggesting the aftermath of rough sex or rape. Swatch watches, popular among young people, feature a poster of a high school couple in bed, apparently unclothed, studying together. Is it any wonder we are plagued by teen promiscuity?

The widespread moral abuse of our kids makes appropriate sex education very difficult and presents us with a critical question: How can we teach our children a biblical view of sex when from a very early age they are inundated with information that directly conflicts with biblical values? As a concerned father, I have searched the Scriptures to answer this question, and I have found there a two-fold strategy for raising kids. God's approach is built on a complimentary relationship between *protection* and *preparation*. Protection involves taking steps to minimize moral threats so our kids have a chance to develop a biblical value system. If we don't protect them, we may lose them before we even have the opportunity to prepare them with spiritual truth.

In the pages that follow I will present the biblical basis for protection and preparation and explain in detail this two-fold strategy. But first, let's take a close-up look at moral abuse so we can better understand the unyielding, sensual oppression impinging on our kids.

THE MORAL ABUSE OF YOUNG CHILDREN

Too Much Too Soon

David Elkind, in his insightful book *The Hurried Child—Growing Up Too Fast Too Soon,* describes the intense pressures our children must face today. Elkind maintains that forcing young children to make adult decisions and value judgments is a form of abuse, which he calls "the abuse of hurrying." Developmental hurrying occurs "whenever we ask children to understand beyond their limits of understanding, to decide beyond their capacity to make decisions or to act willfully before they have the will to act." This abuse threatens their trust, sense of security, and sense of self worth.[1]

**Moral abuse occurs when a young child is confronted
with sexual information that he, by virtue of his
age and inexperience, cannot comprehend.**

When young children are morally assaulted, they suffer from confusion which produces deep-seated anxieties and profound insecurities. Their young minds cannot comprehend information presented by an increasingly sick adult world.

As if combating the media and other merchants of sex is not enough, our own neighbors can pose an even greater threat. One mother told me of an episode that many parents have had to face:

> When my son was four years old, he was playing at a friend's house, and I just happened to be downstairs visiting with the mother. We went to check on the boys because they were so quiet. When we got there, we couldn't find them at first. When we did, they had all their clothes off. We asked them what they were doing—why they had their clothes off. The other little boy picked up an open magazine from his bed and showed it to his mother. Her face was horror stricken. The picture showed several people with no clothes on in various stages or positions of sexual encounters. Needless to say, we were both shaken. She asked the little boy where he had found it. He took her into his parents' room and in a bottom drawer of his father's dresser showed her a drawer of such books.

Now I don't know if this took place in a Christian home, but I can assure you that incidents such as this do take place in Christian homes. In fact, a mother recently told me that her son who had just entered junior high school saw his first *Playboy* magazine at the home of some friends who profess to be believers and attend a Bible-centered church.

Too Much Too Often

One day I decided to observe carefully the sensual messages assaulting my children in the course of their day. At the grocery store where we do most of our shopping, I parked in the usual place and entered the side door. As soon as I walked in, I came face to face with a mountain of video tapes. I was familiar with the north side of the mountain where the Disney movies could be found. But as I turned from Donald Duck, Mickey Mouse, and Old Yeller, I came face to face with *Maria's Lovers, Great Sex,* and *Going All the Way,* subtitled *Sometimes There's Only One Thing on Your Mind.* Each enticing cover depicted what was to be found on the tape. For example, one movie called *School Spirit* had a girl partially covered with a towel that a young man was about to steal. The copy line read, "Bill is an angel but what he has in mind is absolutely devilish." The angel-demon theme was also captured in the film *Possession— Inhuman Ecstasy Fulfilled.*

As I made my way around this media mountain, I went through the turnstyle that runs alongside the magazine rack. The array of four-color covers almost produced a sensory overload. My eyes were drawn to the scantily clad woman on the front of *Cosmopolitan* who (like the women who pump iron) apparently enjoyed exposing her pectorals.

As I turned from the glare of the glossy covers, I fell into the world of romance novels such as *Strange Sins* and *Flame.* Without the seductive covers, one might have assumed that the first book was written by a preacher and the second by a fireman!

I must admit I had become desensitized until I started to think about how this onslaught influences my own children. By the time I left, I had a renewed sensitivity to the sexually suggestive messages that are now commonplace in our neighborhood grocery stores and local malls.

The next time you go shopping, start observing with your child's perspective in mind. You may be rudely awakened as one woman was:

I went into a card store looking for a gift item. As I passed one of the card racks, a card titled Oral Sex stood out like a sore thumb. Bold orange 3/4" lettering on white background . . . you couldn't miss it. One would expect this sort of thing in an adult bookstore but certainly not in a neighborhood gift shop. That card and the others were well within reach of any child who could read. It is little wonder that our young people are so insecure, so mixed up with no feelings of direction. They don't need this kind of sex education. They need censorship in the worst way. Adults are making BIG BUCKS at the expense of our youth while we parents sit back totally apathetic allowing this to happen in our movies, books, music, magazines, TV programming, and even in our telephones.

In your mind's eye, watch as your little six-year-old girl, who is just learning to read, sees the card described above. She stares at the bright letters and tries to sound out the words, o-r-a-l. Then, she turns and asks you what the card means. Or imagine that it's your sixteen-year-old daughter who is being pressured by her boyfriend to have oral sex. She sees the card, knows what it means, and relaxes her moral guard as she concludes that anything displayed so openly can't be all that wrong.

Have you ever thought about what happens in the mental computer of children inundated with explicit material and our society's view of sex? When they see a news clip of homosexual lovers kissing while one lies in a hospital ward dying of AIDS . . . when they hear a popular song that sings of safe sex . . . when unmarried and apparently unclothed lovers embrace in a steamy bedroom scene . . . what goes through our kids' minds? Or scarier yet, what images will remain, misinforming young minds about sex and relationships and inviting them to engage in acts they would have never imagined on their own?

THE MORAL ABUSE OF TEENAGERS

**Moral abuse occurs when a child's understanding
and moral defenses are overwhelmed by exposure
to explicit sexual information and ethical challenges.**

Profound Changes and Sexual Education

Whether we like it or not, our children will be forced to respond to information that was not even available to us when we were their age. From a Christian perspective, this fact is disturbing enough. But even secularists such as Jane Norman and Myron Harris see this shift as nothing short of overwhelming:

The resulting changes in sexual values and practices may seem outrageous to some adults, but to our teenagers the so-called sexual revolution is a fact of life. They grew up at its height—in a time of open nudity in magazines and movies; of legalized abortions; of unmarried couples living together; of birth-control pills; of X-rated movies.

They see their divorced parents date and bring lovers home for the night. Some kids have seen their parents swap partners, and some have lived with a number of sets of parents as a result of this mate exchange.

Sex is constantly being examined clinically on the radio, television, and in countless books and magazines. Masturbation, clitoral stimulation, and multiple orgasms are no longer terms used only by sex therapists.

What effect has all this had on our teenagers' sexual behavior and attitudes?

Teens are sexually active at a younger age, some having intercourse as early as eleven years old. They are getting pregnant and having abortions as never before. Many, however, are electing to keep their babies and remain unmarried. A large percentage of young people expect to live with someone before getting married. Some admit to being bisexual, and many more homosexual.

There will probably never be a return to the preteen white dresses with pink sashes. Both girls and boys are dressing as sex symbols in their skintight designer jeans, even in prepuberty. Madison Avenue has created enticingly erotic ads and commercials that sell sexuality as part of the total dress package. Soap operas, movies, and television programs do not hesitate to dramatize previously taboo subjects such as rape, abortion, and incest.

There is no doubt that our teenagers feel freer to discuss and act upon their sexual proclivities in these liberal times.[2]

David Elkind, a sociologist, sees how teens are now fair game for sexual enticement:

In today's rapidly changing society, teenagers have lost their once privileged position. Instead, they have had a premature adulthood thrust upon them. Teenagers now are expected to confront life and its challenges with the maturity once expected only of the middle-aged, without any time for preparation. Many adults are too busy retooling and retraining their own job skills to devote any time to preparing the next generation of workers. And some parents are so involved in reordering their own lives, managing a career, marriage, parenting, and leisure, that they have no time to give their teenagers; other parents simply cannot train a teenager for an adulthood they themselves have yet to attain fully. The media and merchandisers, too, no longer abide by the unwritten rule that teenagers are a privileged group who require special protection and nurturing. They now see teenagers as fair game for all the arts of persuasion and sexual innuendo once directed only to adult audiences and consumers. High schools, which were once the setting for a unique teenage culture and language, have become miniatures of the adult community. Theft, violence, sex, and substance abuse are now as common in the high schools as they are on the streets.[3]

Moral Absolutes Abandoned

The rapid changes that have occurred in our society challenge the emotional stability of *all* teenagers, but these changes have a particularly profound impact on *Christian* kids and their families.

By "Christian home" I mean a family in which mom or dad or both have a personal relationship with Jesus Christ. The parents are not merely churchgoers but are committed to operating their family life according to the Word of God. Kids who grow up in Christ-centered homes soon discover that many people ridicule Christian values as prudish and archaic. Before long they sense they are the rope in a tug of war with their parents and church on one end and their friends and everyone else on the other.

Our society has dismissed absolute standards for a person's behavior. This has occurred on several fronts, including public school textbooks such as Prentice Hall's third edition of *Health,* which reads:

> Ancient Christians and Jews considered abortion a sin against God's commandments and his wish for man to 'be fruitful and multiply.'
>
> The fear of underpopulation, however, has reversed itself—the world is rapidly becoming overpopulated. For this reason, many

people have come to regard birth control and abortion as the only viable alternatives to a disastrously overcrowded environment.

The liberalized abortion laws have led to a sharp decrease in the number of abortion-related deaths. . . . In fact, legal abortions are much safer than childbirth. . . .

In addition, pregnancy and childbirth are far more expensive than abortion; and it is impossible to measure the psychological harm caused by having an unwanted child.[4]

Picture your teen sitting in the classroom reading that "ancient Christians" considered abortion a sin. The implications are that even "modern Christians" no longer view abortion this way and that anyone holding these archaic values is out of step. In just a few sentences, "You shall not murder" is discarded for population control, personal safety, cost, and convenience.

This, once again, is a form of moral abuse. We teach our children one standard, and the schools teach an opposing one. Impressionable young minds are then left to make decisions on ethical questions they cannot fully understand.

How many slams can a Christian kid take before he begins to question his parents' scripturally based standards? Believe me, it doesn't take long, especially when biblical values are undermined long before we have a chance to equip our kids with adequate answers.

Parental Authority Assaulted

Imagine that your fifteen-year-old daughter gets pregnant. Fearful of telling you, she goes to the local bookstore and buys *Changing Bodies, Changing Lives: A Book for Teens on Sex and Relationships*. She sneaks the book up into her room and closes the door. With tears in her eyes, she turns to the section called "Deciding whether to have an abortion." Then she reads:

The decision to have an abortion is yours as the pregnant girl. *No one can force you to have one if you don't want to*. No doctor, clinic or hospital can legally do an abortion unless they have *your written consent. Don't sign anything until you read it first, and if you don't understand the language, ask to have it explained to you until you do understand.*

The Supreme Court has ruled that minors (people under eighteen) can get an abortion without parental consent. Some doctors and clinics require parental consent anyway if you are a minor. These places are afraid of lawsuits brought on by angry parents. If getting your parents' consent will be a problem for you, ask the people at the clinic when you call for an appointment if they require written parental consent before performing abortions on minors. Many places will perform simple abortions (when you are *under* twelve weeks pregnant) without parental consent.[5]

She keeps reading and finds out that others will help her protect her legal rights to have an abortion no matter what her parents or family doctor have to say:

If you have any questions about your rights or if you believe a doctor or clinic has violated your rights, call the National Abortion Federation at 1-800-223-0618. That is a toll-free number, so it will not cost you anything. If you live in New York City, call 688-8516. You may also call your local chapter of the American Civil Liberties Union (ACLU), a local chapter of the National Organization of Women (NOW) or Planned Parenthood.[6]

The Supreme Court, with a simple stroke of the pen, told our kids they do not have to obey us as parents. In fact, they don't even have to consult with us on the potentially life-shattering decision to have an abortion. Other adults with law books in hand will come to our kid's defense if we oppose our teenager's choice to kill her unborn baby.

Our suicidal system has contributed to the moral abuse of our kids by lifting the anchor of parental control and allowing young people to float aimlessly in the troubled seas of our day.

Our God-ordained authority as parents is no longer respected in the courts of our land, and our kids know it. A sixteen-year-old boy from a Christian home became enthralled with a group of punk rockers. When his parents objected, he warned them that in a few months, when he turned seventeen, they couldn't do a thing to stop him. He left home on that day. The next time his parents saw him was when they bailed him out of jail for possession of narcotics.

The legal climate in our country often encourages our kids to rebel whenever we assert any authority. Fearing such rebellion, many of us allow our kids simply to conform to the world in which they live. Unfortunately, when we do so we may be causing them to sin.

CAUSING A CHILD TO SIN

A Goliath of sexual misinformation and immorality threatens our children's very lives. This warrior's arsenal of weapons—television, movies, music, magazines, books, schools, legal authorities, and peer pressure—seem to make him omnipresent and invincible. But like the Goliath of old who faced a shepherd boy named David and fell dead from the blow of a single small stone, today's Goliath can also meet his match if we confront him with the weapons I describe in the chapters that follow.

Moreover, we can find courage and consolation in the fact that this warring giant will not even have the ultimate victory. Jesus Christ promised as much in an answer He gave to His disciples. When they asked Him who would be the greatest in the kingdom of heaven, He called to a little child to come stand among them. Then He pointed out that the simple faith of a child is what makes someone great in God's kingdom. But He didn't stop there. He went on to explain how children should be treated and what would happen to those who caused them to sin: "And whoever welcomes a little child like this in my name welcomes me. But if anyone causes one of these little ones who believe in me to sin, it would be better for him to have a large millstone hung around his neck and to be drowned in the depths of the sea. Woe to the world because of the things that cause people to sin! Such things must come, but woe to the man through whom they come!" (Matt. 18:5–7).

The Greek term for *little child* refers to children between the ages of four and twelve. Adults who help them understand the gospel message and trust in Christ for their salvation are pleasing Him. But those who lead children astray are in danger of falling under a severe judgment.

Jesus emphasized this fact by using an illustration that would have been abundantly clear to His audience. In His day, millstones were used for grinding corn, and they came in two sizes. One was small enough to be used by hand. The larger size was so huge and heavy that only oxen or a group of slaves could move it. Jesus had this bigger stone in mind when He spoke about causing a child to sin. Anyone who makes a child go wrong will be punished by God so severely that it would be better if a large millstone were tied around his neck and he be dumped in the deepest part of the sea to suffer the agony of drowning. In God's eyes, people who force children to make premature ethical decisions deserve stringent retribution—even to the point of physical or spiritual death. God will not let them get away with their crime: " 'It is mine to avenge; I will repay,' says the Lord" (Rom. 12:19).

So we can challenge our Goliath with the same confidence young David had when he went up against his Goliath. He knew that God would help him defeat the foe (1 Sam. 17:37). The Lord will do the same for us.

So join me as we search the Scriptures for God's solution to our Goliath problem.

GIVE IT SOME THOUGHT

1. What pressures does your child face that you didn't have while growing up?

2. In your mind, walk through a typical day with your child. What are the sources of your child's sexual information?

3. What moral options does your child commonly face?

4. What are the long-term effects of moral abuse on your child?

5. Is your child sexually active?

CHAPTER 4

The Priority of Protection

"Coach" didn't have any children, so his little league baseball team became his family. His life revolved around his players; there wasn't anything he wouldn't do for any of us. I was eight years old when he began picking me up for practices and games. Whenever I needed a ride, he would drive miles out of his way to make sure I could be with the team. He was a friend who really cared about me.

That's why I was excited when he asked me to join him to see the premiere of a new movie in downtown Philadelphia. Coach suggested we take the bus over one Saturday morning and return Saturday night. When I told my mother about the plan, she said point blank, "No!" When I asked why not, she refused to give me an answer. The more I complained, the tougher she got. I told her she was treating me like a baby. She still didn't budge. I decided that if she was going to destroy my fun, I was going to destroy hers. So for days afterward I gave her grief at every opportunity.

Now I thank God and my mother that she stood her ground despite the pressure I put on her. A number of years ago our local newspaper carried a story about "Coach" that described his history of molesting little boys, many of whom played on his little league baseball team. I could have been a victim of that man's perversion. I considered him someone I could trust. But his covert sexual addiction to young boys made him a potential enemy. My life could have been deeply scarred or even ruined if my mother had not protected me.

As an eight-year-old boy I did not have the capacity to suspect that my coach was a homosexual who would have asked or even forced me to engage in sexual acts that I could not even imagine. He would have confronted me with moral options, compelling me to make decisions long before I had the intellectual, emotional, and spiritual capacity to understand what was happening. If it had not been for my mother's keen awareness and timely intervention, who knows what damage would have been done to me?

Most parents are fully aware of the need to protect their children from sexual molestation. The problem has become front-page news and the topic of network specials—and for good reason. No one wants to see his or her child's face on the side of a milk carton with the caption, "Have you seen me?" But while guarding our children from physical threats, we cannot forget the subtle yet persuasive danger of moral molestation. Our kids cannot comprehend the danger of being inundated with distorted sexual information. That's why our hedge of protection should be not only physical but emotional and spiritual as well.

WE MUST PROTECT OUR CHILDREN

When I was growing up, homosexuality was never presented as a morally viable option. Abortion and contraceptives were illegal and not readily available. Premarital and extramarital sex was frowned upon by most people. How far we have fallen! And in just a few years.

We must do our best to keep outside influences from misdirecting our children. How can we do it? In part, by protecting them. A child cannot understand, much less counter, this whirlpool of immorality. Their anxiety and confusion have led to promiscuity, abortion, drugs, drinking, and even suicide. That's why we parents must take the initiative.

Some of us are reluctant to take steps to protect our children because we have some unanswered questions. What does protection involve? Could it cause our children to rebel? Does protection mean isolation? How far do I go?

These questions and many others will be addressed in this chapter and throughout the book, but first keep in mind that protection is only half the equation. In addition to *protection* there must be systematic *preparation* in God's Word, so that when you relinquish your control over your child, he or she knows how to live biblically in our pagan world. With these two elements in mind, let's begin by examining protection biblically and practically.

PROTECTING YOUR CHILD'S HEART

Bad Company Corrupts Good Character

In the city of Corinth some teachers denied the resurrection of Jesus Christ. In response Paul wrote, "Do not be misled: 'Bad company corrupts good character'" (1 Cor. 15:33). To use a modern expression, one bad apple *will* ruin the whole barrel.

Like some of the Christians in Corinth, our kids' good character and solid beliefs can be corrupted by the company they keep. I have received thousands of letters from parents who witnessed the spiritual demise of their children who had taken up with "bad company." There are exceptions, of course. But I can count on one hand the number of times a Christian kid reversed the trend and had a positive impact on a morally abusive peer.

Our children want and need friends, but they must be the right kind of friends.

Avoid Certain People

The apostle Paul had a profound love and respect for Timothy, his son in the faith (2 Tim. 1:2). Timothy traveled extensively with Paul, was co-sender of six of Paul's letters, and was personally discipled by the gifted apostle. No one could have had a greater opportunity for spiritual growth than Timothy. But despite his spiritual vitality, Paul warned him about certain people: "But mark this: There will be terrible times in the last days. People will be lovers of themselves, lovers of money, boastful, proud, abusive, disobedient to their parents, ungrateful, unholy, without love, unforgiving, slanderous, without self-control, brutal, not lovers of the good, treacherous, rash, conceited, lovers of pleasure rather than lovers of God—having a form of godliness but denying its power. Have nothing to do with them" (2 Tim. 3:1–5).

What an incredibly accurate description of our day. Self-love has become a virtual cult in our country; and we read, "People will be lovers of themselves." We laugh about "yuppies" (young urban professionals) and "dinks" (dual income, no kids) and read, "lovers of money." More and more teens run away from home, and we read that in the last days children will be "disobedient to their parents." Educators, doctors, government officials, and even parents assume teen sex is a given; and we read, "without self-control." AIDS threatens the very existence of modern civilization; we turn to condoms rather than to the Creator; and we read, "lovers of pleasure rather than lovers of God." High-profile religious leaders turn out to be sex-crazed thieves; and we read, "having a form of godliness but denying its power."

How did Paul advise Timothy to respond to these perpetrators of moral abuse? Did he tell him to win them to Christ? No. He told Timothy, "Have nothing to do with them." Was Paul against reaching these people with the gospel? Not at all. In fact, in the next breath he tells Timothy, "Do the work of an evangelist. . ." (2 Tim. 4:5).

How can we explain this tension in Paul's counsel? Very simply. Paul knew that bad company could corrupt Timothy's good character. Intimate involvement with these people could be his downfall. Timothy needed to concentrate on his own spiritual life. That's why the Apostle wrote: "Evil men and impostors will go from bad to worse, deceiving and being deceived. But as for you, continue in what you have learned and have become convinced of. . ." (2 Tim. 3:13, 14).

When a well-trained spiritual giant like Timothy has to be cautioned about corrupt influences, we must get concerned about their impact on our ill-equipped, spiritually immature children.

What was it about these evil men and impostors that concerned Paul? A clue appears earlier in Paul's letter. "Flee the evil desires of youth" (2 Tim. 2:22). Timothy was a young man with strong sexual desires. To control them, he had to limit his contact with individuals who would entice him to sin. He needed to insulate, not isolate, himself from potential tempters.

Insulate, Not Isolate

How much insulation do you have in the walls of your home? How about in the roof? What's the purpose of insulation?

Insulation protects and preserves the atmosphere in the home from outside elements. No matter how much insulation you have, the weather outside will to some degree influence conditions inside. But the insulation allows a degree of security and comfort which promotes good health and growth.

Protection means we insulate our kids from some of the harsh moral climate of our day to give them the opportunity to grow spiritually strong. The more wicked the weather in your community, the greater the need for insulation. If your child is spiritually weak, insulation becomes all the more critical.

Although the apostle Paul repeatedly warned Timothy and others about spiritual contamination (2 Cor. 7:1), he was a pragmatist. He knew that the only way to isolate ourselves from sin and sinners would be to exit the world: "I have written you in my letter not to associate with sexually immoral people—not at all meaning the people of this world who are immoral, or the greedy and swindlers, or idolaters. In that case you would have to leave this world" (1 Cor. 5:9, 10).

Some association with immoral people is inevitable. But our relationship with our unbelieving world is one where we expose what they do, not join in with them. Paul also said, "Have nothing to do with the fruitless deeds of darkness, but rather expose them" (Eph. 5:11). As a father to his grown son, Paul warned Timothy to avoid people whose flagrant lifestyle might undermine his godly purity and commitment to Christ.

Paul simply warned Timothy. We, however, should not only warn our children but also be willing to force their compliance at any cost. Young people, even teenagers, do not normally understand the potential pitfalls of being in bad company. God has given us authority over them, and we should exercise that authority in their best interest.

Association Versus Alliance

Most parents see the need to protect their kids from extremes of moral abuse. They do not want homosexuals teaching their children about alternate lifestyles. They don't want the schools providing condoms. The question then becomes, How far do we go in guarding the spiritual development of our kids?

We have just seen that association with immorality is inevitable.

But what is not inevitable is alliance—becoming tightly knit to immoral people who can lead our kids into spiritual decadence. The Bible warns against forming alliances with unbelievers.

> Do not be yoked together with unbelievers. For what do righteousness and wickedness have in common? Or what fellowship can light have with darkness? What harmony is there between Christ and Belial? What does a believer have in common with an unbeliever? What agreement is there between the temple of God and idols? For we are the temple of the living God. As God has said: "I will live with them and walk among them, and I will be their God, and they will be my people."
> "Therefore come out from them and be separate," says the Lord (2 Cor. 6:14–17).

When you read the word *yoke*, imagine two oxen walking in tandem, harnessed to the same wood frame. Paul used this term to describe a relationship such as we find in marriage, business, or an intimate friendship.

According to this passage, no believer, including our kids, should become closely aligned with an unbeliever. In fact, the differences between Christians and non-Christians are so great that any real, deep relationship where values are shared is impossible. The only way the impossible can be bridged is if the light surrenders to the darkness or the darkness to the light. But they cannot coexist in unity without one overtaking the other.

Like a doctor to his patient, we must get close enough to heal, but not so close as to get the disease we're trying to cure. We must reach out to our unbelieving world, but not at the expense of our own personal purity. We must get close enough to influence non-Christians for their good, but not so close they influence us to our detriment.

Sin Spreads

How important is it that our kids *not* get closely involved with their immoral peers? It is so important that God warns us even to avoid believers who are not living what they profess.

In dealing with the problem of incest in the Corinthian church,

Paul set forth the principle that sin spreads. "Don't you know that a little yeast works through the whole batch of dough?" (1 Cor. 5:6). In other words, sin will spread through the whole church unless its source is removed. Bad company *will* corrupt good character.

With this principle in mind, Paul went a step further: "But now I am writing you that you must not associate with anyone who calls himself a brother but is sexually immoral or greedy, an idolater or a slanderer, a drunkard or a swindler. With such a man do not even eat" (1 Cor. 5:11). Some commentators suggest that Paul wanted the Corinthians to avoid people who were under church discipline. If that were the case, then church discipline should also be administered for greed, idolatry, slander, drunkenness, and swindling, in addition to sexual immorality.

Regardless, the point is clear. Sin is contagious, even among Christians.

Now, an even tougher question: How do we apply these principles to our children and their friendships?

Parents Versus Peers

The mental diary of my own childhood recalls a tug of war between accepting my parents' standards and wanting to be accepted by my teenage classmates. They were often in direct conflict. My parents certainly didn't want me to drink, but my friends invited me to weekend beer parties. My parents didn't want me to have a physical relationship with my girlfriend, but my buddies told me about their sexual escapades with their girlfriends. There I stood, caught in the crossfire of conflicting values. Today, the peer pressure to drink, do drugs, and engage in premarital sex has become a vice grip around the throats of our children.

Most parents do not understand the inner turmoil of a child confronted with the choice to reject mom and dad's standards. The invitation typically comes from a friend in the form of a challenge to do something wrong in the name of personal freedom and independence. Motivated by a profound desire to be accepted, illicit behavior suddenly becomes a summons to conform. What can a parent do to counter the potentially overwhelming influence of a child's friends?

By nature of their vulnerability, children will be influenced by others. Biblically speaking, parental influences should outweigh any other natural force in a child's life. Not to impinge, but to impact. Not to destroy, but to direct. Yes, one day we must relinquish control, but not to a group of misdirected teenagers trapped between adolescence and adulthood. Where parental control ends, control by the Holy Spirit must begin.

Let me offer several practical ways you can counter negative peer pressure.

1. Be careful not to alienate your child by inconsistent or harsh discipline.

2. Maintain relational leverage with your child by investing the time necessary to develop real intimacy.

3. Know your child's strengths and weaknesses. Is your child a leader or a follower? How strong are his sexual desires? How far has she gone sexually?

4. Know your child's friends. Create opportunities to see her friends firsthand. Have them spend the night at your home. Listen to their conversations while driving them in the car.

5. Encourage friendships with other young people who respect authority and share your spiritual sensitivities.

6. Arm your child with ways to combat negative peer pressure. Some young people can be taught to give a strong verbal defense, while others should be encouraged to simply walk away from their peers' moral assaults.

7. If all else fails, move. If you sense you are losing your child and other methods have not worked, relocation may be necessary. Consider one family's experience: "Our son was raised in a Christian home. We moved across town, which isolated him from his friends at church. He began to attend a secular junior high school and befriended the new punk-rock neighbors next door. His Sunday attendance at church could not combat the 35 hours of secular influence at school and secular friends. He fell into great sin. We had to move away from the neighbors and put him in a Christian school to begin to get his old loving self back."

Granted, we cannot move every time our child's faith is challenged. But when it becomes obvious we are losing our son or daughter, we must take whatever steps are necessary to restore his or her relationship with the Lord, regardless of the cost.

PROTECTING YOUR CHILD'S MIND

As Your Child Thinks

Biblical protectionism also involves the mind. This is where many Christian young people are losing the battle. We are permitting them to feed their minds with impure thoughts that eventually produce impure actions. With their minds focused on earthly things and not on "things above" (Col. 3:2), they are not prepared to respond biblically (1 Pet. 1:13) and end up living according to their sin nature (Rom. 8:5).

The Bible never says we should engage our minds in mental warfare with immorality. Instead, it says, "Whatever is true, whatever is noble, whatever is right, whatever is pure, whatever is lovely, whatever is admirable—if anything is excellent or praiseworthy—think about such things" (Phil. 4:8). Since our kids are just learning about what is true, noble, right, pure, lovely, admirable, and praiseworthy, we must help them to protect their minds. They don't know any better. We do, or at least we should.

Flee Temptation

God's Word repeatedly warns us to protect ourselves (and by implication our kids) from people and situations where we will be tempted to sin. The whole concept of distancing ourselves from invitations to sin supports the idea of protection. We are told to "flee from sexual immorality" (1 Cor. 6:18). Paul told Timothy, "Flee the evil desires of youth. . ." (2 Tim. 2:22).

James makes it clear that our God has nothing to do with the temptations so prevalent in our day: "When tempted, no one should say, 'God is tempting me.' For God cannot be tempted by evil, nor does he tempt anyone; but each one is tempted when, by his own evil desire, he is dragged away and enticed. Then, after desire has conceived, it gives birth to . . . death" (James 1:13–15).

These words picture a fisherman who, having carefully baited his hook, tosses it into a pond and invites the response of the fish. When they get close, he tugs on the line to heighten their desire and invite further pursuit. More and more fish gather, drawing closer and closer to the bait. A couple of fish not only get close but actually nibble on the bait. When they get away unscathed, others decide it's safe and venture closer for a tasty treat. Then, in a split second, it happens. The hook plants itself in the mouth of the now unsuspecting fish. The pleasure of the bait gives way to the pain of the hook.

That's the scenario that threatens our kids as they encounter the baited hooks of sensual enticements. Rather than flee, they nibble away at explicit information until their desires conceive a thought or a plan that ends in sexual sin.

When I consider the programs and movies some parents permit their children to watch, I am amazed we don't have an even greater problem with teens and preteens biting the hook of promiscuity. When you consider the skimpy bathing suits teenage girls wear, is it any wonder our kids are on hormonal overload? On a beach in Galveston, my family saw a young couple probably fifteen or sixteen years of age; the girl had on a bathing suit that was no more than an inch wide at any place. No normal young person can handle such temptation for very long. That's why we must help them and teach them how to protect themselves from compromise.

When we let our kids expose themselves to material even adults would have trouble handling, then turn around and act surprised that they are failing sexually, we're behaving as foolishly as the man who poured gasoline on a fire and voiced disbelief over the fact that it fueled the flames rather than snuffed them out. We can't fuel our children's passions, then expect our kids to keep a tight grip on them until marriage. But if we provide an environment in which their sexual drives can be controlled and properly directed, we will have greatly reduced the threat of sexual temptation.

Of course, we can't keep our eyes on our kids at all times. That wouldn't be healthy for us or our kids. But if we protect them by putting adequate distance between them and the source of temptation and if we teach them how to recognize and deal with situations that threaten to compromise their purity, we go a long way toward helping them avoid falling prey to the lures of temptation. When they are younger, we demand they distance themselves from sexual temptation. By the time they reach the late teens, they should fully understand the need to protect themselves from compromising situations.

The Trouble with Television

As I was growing up in the Nieder household, our television was treated as a member of the immediate family. It served as the centerpiece of family activities.

One day when the TV tube burned out, only a funeral dirge would have captured our emotion. Fortunately, or tragically, we were able to locate an appropriate donor, who allowed us to successfully perform an intricate tube transplant.

Withdrawal pains that occurred then were resurrected years later when I challenged some local friends to turn off their televisions for just one week to test for cathode ray addiction. After two days I started to receive obscene phone calls from frustrated fanatics who needed a fix. Some wanted to know if religious programs were exempt. I told them only for income tax purposes. Several asked if the all-star game came under a special dispensation.

When we broadcast the same challenge on our radio program, we were inundated with mail from the families of TV addicts as well as from those who had been detoxed.

Even a casual observer of the TV, video, and film curriculum recognizes the profound influence of the plug-in drug. Everyone from laborers to lawyers can be mesmerized by its message. A marketing executive who understands the media far better than I ever will gave me his perspective:

> I was interested in the one-week time frame you asked your people to go without TV. We experienced about one month of serious withdrawal pains; and I use the term withdrawal because in fact TV is an addiction, just like drugs or what have you. After one month the pain started slowly tapering off until after a few months the healing was complete.
>
> That was about 13 years ago. At this time our family would not even consider having a TV in our home, even if it were the best model available and were given to us free. We recognize TV for what it is . . . the "eye and mouth of Satan." Now that may sound a little bit fanatical, but consider it in light of the fact that no other communication medium in existence espouses more the philosophies of the Adversary and puts down more the Word of God! I am firmly con-

vinced that more harm has been done to the cause of our Lord through TV than through any other action, any place, ever.

As a marketing executive, I am thoroughly familiar with the power and purposes of the media, whether it be the TV, radio, or written material. As you know, the purpose of the media is to develop an audience that can be sold to advertisers. In addition to the fact that the programming appeals to our natural lusts, there is also a psychological hook that visual media uses to "demand" our attention. Because of these considerations, Christians should recognize that TV is really a very dangerous thing to have in the home; it's akin to having a loaded gun lying around in easy reach of our children.

When the average child watches three hours and one minute of television each day and the typical teen three hours and two minutes, is it any wonder they are buying into the secular world? In the American home the TV is on for seven hours and five minutes a day with adults averaging four hours and nineteen minutes of viewing.[1] Is it any wonder most Christians are conforming to the world rather than to God's Word?

Our spiritual growth and that of our children have been stunted. We have replaced the 23rd Psalm with the 23rd Channel.

> The TV set is my shepherd. My spiritual growth shall want.
> It maketh me to sit down and do nothing for His name's sake,
>   because it requireth all my spare time.
> It keepeth me from doing my duty as a Christian because it
>   presenteth so many shows that I must see.
> It restoreth my knowledge of the things of the world and
>   keepeth me from the study of God's Word.
> It leadeth me in the paths of failing to attend the evening
>   services.
> Yea, though I live to be a hundred, I shall keep on viewing my
>   TV as long as it will work, for it is my closest companion.
> Its sound and its picture, they comfort me.
> Surely, no good things will come of my life, because my TV
>   offereth no good time to do the will of God;
> thus I will dwell in my TV room forever.

If we don't compel our children to turn off the TV or to control its use carefully, we might as well invite Hollywood into our homes to teach our children about sex and everything else.

Someone might suggest that parents view television programs with their children to point out and discuss the non-Christian attitudes and actions they depict. For a great number of programs, all you would do is point and discuss, point and discuss. Now I heartily recommend that children learn to grapple with our society from a Christian perspective. But allowing massive amounts of moral garbage into their minds will not teach them a biblical world view or biblical discernment. What it will do is allow the world to sell them its view no matter what we say or do.

TAME IT OR TRASH IT

And so we come to the big question: How do you "compel" a child to tame or trash the TV? First of all, you begin with the conviction that this is in the best interest of your child. Remember, you have the God-given authority and responsibility to do what is best for your child. Second, don't ask your child to do anything you are not willing to do. If you want him to turn off the trash—you do the same. Third, explain from a biblical perspective why we must monitor our viewing of television, videos, and movies. Fourth, offer some exciting and creative alternatives. Play board games, throw the ball, go hiking, ride bikes, and just enjoy being together. And finally, decide to tame or trash the television. One family told me they attached a VCR to a computer monitor which gave them complete control over what their children watched.

I suspect you fear that telling your child to turn off the TV will eternally ruin your relationship. Before you reach that conclusion, read two letters I received from some young people. The first letter comes from Debbie in Topeka, Kansas: "I am 12 years old and I was listening to your radio program about TV. My family recently put the TVs in their boxes. My mom said our lives just revolve around TV. Since there are so many bad things on, I'm glad I can spend more time with my family and listen to the nice Christian programs on radio."

The next letter came from a young woman in her twenties. As

you read, think of your child years from now, wishing that you had helped him or her to turn off the tube.

"Television was a very big part of my life during my school years. From the moment I arrived home from school until the time I went to sleep, I sat in front of a TV. I ate my meals in front of the TV. I did my homework in front of the TV. Sometimes I simply 'vegetated' in front of the TV. My week's activities were scheduled around those TV programs that I *had* to watch. TV literally ran my life.

"Through my college years I watched less TV, yet my life still was centered around this program and that. I was, at this point, a new Christian, and I missed out on some wonderful opportunities because of my need to constantly be filled with exciting and glamorous lifestyles which could only be found through television.

"Finally, during my last semester at the college, I sold my TV, not fully realizing the impact that the decision would have. For the first time in my life, I had 'spare' time. That was something I seemed never before to have. I suddenly had time for people. I had time for myself. And most importantly, I had time for the Lord. The Lord and I can now spend many wonderful hours together— hours that had once belonged to my 'TV-god.' And I do praise God for showing me just how wonderful He is—something I may never have learned if I were still under the influence of TV.

"I have been without television now for 2 months. In its place God has put wonderful Christian radio programs and music, as well as time with people. He has also given me very special times in prayer and in His wonderful Word. I have absolutely no desire whatsoever for television now. My only desire is to be close to my wonderful Creator.

"It may take a lifetime of being without television to 'undo' the harm that was caused by TV in the first place, but praise God, because now I am truly free."

Does God want us to protect our children from morally misdirected influences coming through television, videos, and movies? Absolutely. Beyond a doubt. In fact, He wants all believers to take certain precautions to avoid illicit allurement. Considering the vulnerability of naive kids, the biblical admonitions are all the more critical and pertinent. And we need to apply them not only to friendships and the media but also to what takes place in our child's school.

THE EDUCATIONAL OPTIONS

Where should my child go to school? The answer to this question has become increasingly difficult because of the dramatic changes in our schools. In a cover story entitled "Getting Tough," *Time* magazine cited a study which compared school discipline problems from forty years ago with today.[2] The comparison is shocking:

SCHOOL DISCIPLINE PROBLEMS	
1940s	1980s
Talking	Drug abuse
Chewing gum	Alcohol abuse
Making noise	Pregnancy
Running in the hallways	Suicide
	Rape
Getting out of place in line	Robbery
	Assault
Wearing improper clothing	Burglary
	Arson
Not putting paper in wastebaskets	Bombings

For these changes alone, we cannot ignore the educational options available to our children, and we must not fail to pick the best one for them.

There are essentially four possible approaches to educating our children: the public schools, private secular schools, private Christian schools, and home schools. Some parents sense they do not have a choice and feel compelled to send their children to the public school. Other parents have both the financial resources and the availability of a private secular or Christian school. Homeschooling by design is a ready option and is relatively inexpensive.

Evaluating these school environments and making the right decision for your child goes beyond the scope of this book. But, in view of our discussion of moral abuse, a critical question must be answered: Can my child not only survive but thrive in the spiritual jungle of the public school system? Some young people can, but a great many cannot. Some schools have been strongly influenced by Christian teachers and some have not. That's why we as parents must be students of our kids as well as the local public school they may attend. There was a day when the Judeo-Christian ethic permeated the academic environment of our schools. Although it still exists in some schools, it has become a rare commodity in most.

I have talked with some of the most respected Christian educators in our country who sent their now-grown kids to the local public schools. I have asked them if they would do the same today. The usual answer is no. One man likened it to the ancient Israelites sending their children to a school taught by the pagan Canaanites. Another told me that all the problems we see today existed years ago in isolated cases, but now the immorality is so widespread he would not consider enrolling his children in public schools.

Private schools, Christian schools, and home schools are viable options for many parents. There are pros and cons to each alternative. For those who can attend, private secular schools may offer a healthy moral environment where your family's values, although not reinforced, will not be undermined. Christian schools that emphasize character as much as the curriculum can be an excellent educational alternative. Unfortunately, the expense may be prohibitive for many families.

Homeschooling has become the choice of a growing number of parents who want to spend more time with their kids, following the model presented in Deuteronomy 6. Parents of younger children have opted for homeschooling because it allows children more time to mature spiritually and socially before facing the intense peer pressure in private and public schools.

It is sobering to think that no matter where we send our kids, the responsibility to raise them in the nurture and the admonition of the Lord is ours and not the schools'. This raises one more issue we have to address before moving on.

MISSIONARIES TO SPIRITUAL HEADHUNTERS

I have met a number of Christian parents who have a deep-seated resistance to the thought of monitoring or countering the moral atmosphere surrounding their kids. I suspect it stems from already being on emotional overload. We are fighting to keep body and soul together, and one more worry could test our sanity.

Apart from your own physical limitations, you may have a biblically based objection to the idea of protection. I can almost hear you asking, Shouldn't we be the salt of the earth and the light of the world (Matt. 5:13–16)? If we guard our kids, won't we be losing our saltiness and hiding our light? Shouldn't they be missionaries to their friends and to the public schools? What about Daniel and his three friends in Babylon? Didn't they stand up for their values in a pagan society and win?

Let me respond with several questions. When John the Baptist spent over twenty-five years in the desert before he appeared publicly, was he hiding the light (Luke 1:80)? When Jesus Christ spent the first thirty years of His life in Nazareth studying the Scriptures and working with Joseph in the carpentry shop, was He overprotected? When Timothy spent years at home studying the Scriptures with his mother and grandmother, did he eventually rebel (1 Tim. 3:14–15)? When the apostle Paul stayed in Damascus for several years, growing "more and more powerful" and waiting to take his first missionary trip, was he disobeying God (Acts 9:22, Gal. 1:17–18)?

We would be naive and foolhardy to assume that conversion alone guarantees a person will be a moral preservative or a beacon of light. What's required is spiritual growth that takes time and training, which is exactly what our children need.

"But what about Daniel and his three friends in captivity in Babylon? They were probably in their late teens and they stood their guard!" You are absolutely right. But they were trained in orthodox Jewish homes. Their childhood experience revolved around the Scriptures. They learned to read from the Old Testament. They memorized huge portions of the Scriptures. If we trained our children the way they trained theirs, I would say, "Bring on Babylon." But our kids are typically not ready for our modern Babylon of humanistic thinking and hedonistic values.

The bottom line is this: *Most Christian kids are not ready to rescue their drowning friends.* They do not have the understanding or vitality to fight the undertow pulling their friends out to sea. In fact, if they attempt to rescue them unprepared, they will likely go under too. That's why we must protect them for a short time as we train them for a lifetime.

Protection comes at a price. And at times it will be very expensive. Meanwhile, parental energy happens to be a limited commodity with most moms and dads running on empty.

But we will pay—either now or later. If we pay now, we can fall totally exhausted into the empty nest and lie there confident we did our best. We fought a good fight. If we decide to pay later, it may be with some deep regrets that we didn't do more.

With a plan of protection in place, it's now time to prepare your child to face our morally abusive world. In the pages that follow, we will see how.

GIVE IT SOME THOUGHT

1. What is the greatest threat to your child's spiritual development? How can you counter it? Take a few moments to lay out at least a tentative plan.

2. Which of your child's friends is most likely to have a negative impact on him or her? In what ways can you reduce that child's corrupting influence?

3. Which of your child's friends exert positive influence? How can you use them to help your child grow up in Christ?

4. Do you feel you should tame or trash the TV? How will you do it? What creative alternatives can you offer?

5. Who has more relational leverage with your child, you or his peers?

6. What specific steps can you take to improve your relationship with your son or daughter?

CHAPTER 5

The Process of Preparation

My eyes were filled with tears as I walked away from the hospital. The parking lot was empty, but I was not alone. With each step, my heart and my lips poured out the words, "Thanks, Lord. Thank You for my son. Thank You for this special gift."

As part of the new generation of dads, I had coached my wife through the birthing process, and I do mean process. Twenty-seven hours worth. After about twenty hours, I suggested we call it quits and try another day. But Teri refused to leave the hospital without a baby, so she continued to push and I continued to coach. It wasn't until I saw his little head for the first time that I really believed someone had been swimming in there for the past nine months.

Witnessing the birth of my son gave me a renewed appreciation for my mother and all she had endured to bring me into the world. But it didn't prepare me to be a father. My exhilaration and joy soon turned to wonder as I pondered where in the world this kid had come from and what I should do with him now that he was here. Fortunately, Teri wore maternal magnificence from the moment of conception, which bought me some much needed time to work through my own identity crisis.

What does it mean to be a father, a mother, a parent? What's my role? What's my responsibility? After years of struggling, I am just beginning to understand the unique privilege God has given to me—the choice opportunity to take my child's hand and, over a period of eighteen years, place it in His hand.

THE GOAL OF PARENTING

The apostle John captured the purpose of parenting in his third epistle when, thinking of his spiritual children, he wrote, "I have no greater joy than to hear that my children are walking in the truth" (v. 4). We are to do all we can to see that our children walk in the truth, taking each and every step in a close, loving relationship with Jesus Christ. And that naturally requires that our children know the truth. If they don't, how can they live it? If they don't *know* what God says, how can they *do* what He says?

Several years ago at a conference, my friend and mentor, Dr. Howard Hendricks, made a statement that has disturbed me ever since. Out of his vast experience and research, he had discovered that "four out of five children currently enrolled in the educational program of evangelical churches will not be there through the teen years." His conclusion: "We are not reaching kids, nor are we retaining them."

As a parent the question *Why?* gnaws at my soul. Why are so many young people from Christian homes turning away from the faith? I know there must be dozens of reasons, but one dominates my thinking. I believe we are failing to teach our children what it means to walk with Jesus Christ. We want them to have a growing relationship with Him. We tell them to align their lives with His. But we rarely if ever explain how to grow spiritually. That's where we let our kids down. Our biggest concern should be that they come to know Christ personally and flourish in their relationship with Him.

In ancient Lystra there lived a couple who had a young son named Timothy. His mother and grandmother, who were believers, taught him how to walk with God. The apostle Paul then took Timothy under his wing and loved him as his son in the faith (Acts 16:1–3).

Years later, Paul reminded Timothy of who had laid the foundation of his spiritual development and ministry: "But as for you, continue in what you have learned and have become convinced of, because you know those from whom you learned it, and how from infancy you have known the holy scriptures" (2 Tim. 3:14–15).

This small passage could be an entire chapter in a parenting textbook. It tells us that very young children—even toddlers—can learn the Bible. It also points out that those who teach the Scriptures play a very important role. Paul knew that when Timothy remembered his mother and grandmother reading him the Word, he would recall how they modeled its message.

This slice of reality about Timothy gives us two parenting objectives to help us accomplish the goal of seeing our children walk in the truth. Note well that Paul wrote, "What you have learned and been convinced of. . . ." Content and challenge are the crucial components. Timothy not only knew what God said; he personally became convinced of what God said. He not only learned the Scriptures; he decided to live them. Why? Because his mother and grandmother taught him the content of the faith and challenged him to live by that faith. They left nothing to chance. Nothing to peers. Nothing to the church. Nothing to itinerant preachers, speakers, or teachers. Timothy's mother and grandmother took it upon themselves to impart and model the message they wanted him to accept and apply. The result? A man of God on whom the greatest missionary of the church could depend. A man of deep faith. A friend Paul longed to see.

We must combine *education* and *exhortation* if we are going to equip our children for the battles they will face in the years ahead. Candidly, most of us fail to do either of these very well. We really don't know how to teach children, and when we fail to teach them, we certainly have no solid platform from which to challenge them.

What is the source of our problem? It seems to be a product of our busy schedules and the information age in which we live. Most of us know more about computers than we do about Jesus Christ. We typically have not invested the time and energy needed to be knowledgeable of God's Word. So what's the solution? It's multi-faceted, and it's timeless. It's found in the book Jesus quoted most: Deuteronomy.

GOD'S WORD AND YOUR CHILD

The ancient people of Israel passed the torch of truth from one generation to the next by following the guidelines in Deuteronomy 6:4–9:

Hear, O Israel: The LORD our God, the LORD is one. Love the LORD your God with all your heart and with all your soul and with all your strength. These commandments that I give you today are to be upon your hearts. Impress them on your children. Talk about them when you sit at home and when you walk along the road, when you lie down and when you get up. Tie them as symbols on your hands and bind them on your foreheads. Write them on the doorframes of your houses and on your gates.

Closer examination of this passage reveals both an *intellectual* and a *volitional* component in the process of impressing God's decrees and commandments on the children of Israel. Our children need to know something—these commandments. They also need to do something because commandments by their very nature demand a response.

This training textbook that God gave to Israel offers a wealth of ways to equip our children with the Word of God. But it begins with an assumption prevalent in that day but not in ours. It assumes that people believe God has spoken.

In your heart and mind, do you believe that the Bible is God's Word to us? If someone asked you why you think Scripture is important and relevant for today, would you affirm that "All Scripture is God-breathed and is useful for teaching, rebuking, correcting and training in righteousness, so that the man of God may be thoroughly equipped for every good work" (2 Tim. 3:16-17)? If you are unconvinced that the Bible is the very Word of God, you will never pay the price necessary to equip your child with its message.

Of course, believing in the Bible is one thing, applying it, another. How can we use the God-breathed Scriptures to equip our children?

Teach Your Child to Love God

I want my children to love God with all their hearts, with all their minds, with every ounce of their strength. If they love Him, they will want to obey Him. If they obey Him, they will have rich and rewarding lives.

But how does someone come to love another? The two must first be introduced. Then they must have the opportunity to get to know each other. Where can our children meet God? In our homes, where He lives out His life through us. How can they get to know Him? Through what we say and do.

The renowned Old Testament scholar, Dr. Bruce K. Waltke, recounts a time when these truths were driven home in his experience. "In 1970 I was on a postdoctoral fellowship in Israel. As the Lord directed our steps as a family, we rented an apartment across the hallway from an elderly Jewish couple, both of whom had been taught Hebrew in Boston.

"We quickly struck up a friendship. He was conversant in modern Hebrew, and I was not. So every day we would read modern Hebrew texts together for an hour or two. There are about thirty thousand words in modern Hebrew not found in Biblical Hebrew.

"But if I came across a word I didn't know that was also found in the Hebrew Bible, he would say, 'Bruce, you ought to know that word.' Then he'd cite the entire chapter in Hebrew until he got to the word he was looking for.

"One time I said to this man, now about 75, 'I think you could recite the whole book of Psalms in Hebrew from memory.'

" 'I can.'

" 'How long would it take?' I asked.

" 'Two hours.'

" 'Would you be willing to chant the text while I follow in my Hebrew Bible?'

" 'I'd love it,' he said.

"So I sat down for two hours and he recited the entire text. He never missed a vowel in the entire book of Psalms.

"On another occasion he was taking me through Exodus 21 and 22 from memory to find a word that occurs only three times in the whole Old Testament. I said, 'I think you can recite the entire Torah (Genesis to Deuteronomy) from memory.'

"He said, 'I can.' I didn't challenge him.

"At that time, however, my friend was an atheist. He could recite all the Torah, he could recite all the psalms in the original text, and he didn't even believe in God.

"But as we were leaving Israel and embraced each other, he said to me, 'Bruce, I want you to know I'm now a theist.'

" 'That's wonderful,' I said. 'I could wish you were a Christian, but how did you come to be a theist?'

"He said, 'I saw God alive in your home.' "[1]

Does Jesus Christ live in your home? Does your child see Him through you? If you want your child to live for Him, He must be visible in you.

Live What Your Child Needs to Learn

"These commandments must be on your heart." If we have not accepted God's commandments, neither will our children.

Children naturally believe that what's good for them is good for us. They are right. For example, my wife and I have taught our children that watching television usually wastes time, so if we watch it, we should only view programs that will honor God and be of some use to us. One night when I thought my children were asleep, I turned on the television and suddenly heard this voice from the other room call out, "Hey Dad, why do you watch that junk?" I gave the answer most dads would give, "Your mother wanted to. I was just being nice." Then my wife called out from the kitchen, "The Holy Spirit has spoken!"

If we want our children to live God's way, we must live it too.

Etch God's Word on Your Child's Heart and Mind

The word *impress* means to mark or imprint, to make a noticeable change. In the context of Deuteronomy 6, it means that the message brings about change.

A number of years ago when I served as a youth pastor, I visited Jim, a teenager who, although had come from a broken home, began to grow in his response to God's Word throughout his high school years. After an extended romance with his high school sweetheart, he asked me to conduct their wedding.

In our premarital counseling sessions, Jim and his fiancée told me how they had paid the price for purity so they could give themselves to each other as a wedding gift. Both had been marvelously marked by the message of God's Word.

Weeks before they were married, Jim's construction crew co-workers found out that he was a virgin. In the face of their jokes, this gentle giant told his fellow hard hats about Jesus Christ. His words flew like arrows, cutting deeply into their hardened hearts. Beneath their layers of misguided manhood, they knew he was right.

Although Jim came from a broken home and neither of his parents were Christians, the Word of God revolutionized his life and experience. When Jim found out that God said to wait until marriage to have sex, he did. In fact, he and his fiancée waited five years! The ridicule of his coworkers didn't matter because he knew what pleased God.

Make God's Word Your Authority

"Talk about them. . . ." "Them" refers to the commandments of God. That's what we're to discuss with our kids. Why then do we spend so much of our time talking about things that are far less important? We invest hours discussing sports, movies, school, and work and fail even to mention God's Word.

Let's not give our children anything but the best—the unchanging truth of the Word of God. With this in mind, I recommend that we teach about sex and answer questions primarily from the Bible to encourage our children to look to God as the ultimate authority, not only in their early years, but for their entire lives.

Invest Time in Order to Teach

We are to talk about spiritual principles when we sit at home and when we walk along the road and when we lie down and when we get up. Everywhere and at all times—teach.

This may well be the place where the preparation process breaks down. We don't have enough hours with our children, and the few hours we do have are frantic. In describing the marks of the hurried home, Tim Kimmel points out: "Our hurried lifestyle is a result of taking shortcuts in life. *Since the fall of man in the Garden of Eden, sin has refused to let us rest*. Stripped to its core, sin is 'the desire to have it now.' Sin is the enemy of time. It takes time to be organized. It takes time to meaningfully communicate. It takes time to develop intimate friendships. It takes time to build character in a child."[2]

If we plan to prepare our children, it will take a heavy investment of time and energy. We cannot program a child to learn at our pace and according to our schedule. So when the opportunities do arise, it is critical that we be there and respond. But let me ask, How frequently can those opportunities arise if you and your spouse both work? Unless both of you working is really a matter of survival, make sure you count the cost of a double-barreled income.

Mark Your Child's Spiritual Growth and Commitment

Have you ever made a commitment and in a matter of days . . . even hours . . . failed to honor the decision? I have made numerous commitments to diet and exercise. Then, in what seemed like only seconds, I found myself gorging while proclaiming that Paul said that physical exercise is of little profit. While Paul buffeted his body and made it his slave, I buffet mine at my favorite smorgasboard.

Commitments need to be made, marked, and measured. Made by our children in humility before God. Marked by our attention and memory. Measured by holding our children accountable to keep them.

Let me explain. The people of Israel had ways to mark and measure the commitment of their people, including their children. As families, they marked their commitment to the Scriptures by having portions of them actually hanging on the doorframes of their homes or in leather pouches attached to their foreheads. These phylacteries can be seen even today in Israel. While the biblical admonition to do this could be interpreted as figurative, there is still much we can learn from this and other Jewish practices.

When Jesus was twelve, he traveled in a caravan to Jerusalem to celebrate Passover. While there, he challenged the most knowledgeable rabbis. His spiritual development was marked by the occasion, and his growth was measured by his interaction with the rabbis.

Our young people can drift away from the faith without our even noticing. Over a period of years their interest in spiritual things frequently wanes, but we seldom ask them why. We almost expect them to grow cold, and we discount it as a product of their age. I don't buy that—especially when I read about young men such as David, Daniel, John the Baptist, and Timothy.

David, a simple shepherd boy, used his faith to launch a stone that slew a giant. Daniel, as a young boy, was taken captive in Babylon, but even as a teenager he decided to honor God and not King Nebuchadnezzar. As far as we can tell, John the Baptist accepted the personal sacrifice of his Nazarite vow and never rebelled. There is no indication that Timothy, who was living at home when he was recruited by Paul, ever rejected his spiritual heritage.

I would like to offer you two things you can do that can help mark your child's spiritual growth and development. First of all, celebrate his spiritual birthday . . . the most important day in your child's life, far more significant than the physical birthday. Physical birth gives us on the average seventy plus years. Spiritual birth gives us an eternity with God and each other.

In our home we celebrate spiritual birthdays just as we do physical birthdays, usually with a special family evening. We go to one of our favorite places to eat. We talk about what it is was like when we came to know Jesus as Savior. In my wife's case, she became a Christian at a very young age. Because she doesn't know the exact date, we have chosen a day to celebrate her relationship with the Lord.

The year after my son became a Christian, on his first spiritual birthday, I videotaped my memories of that wonderful day. When he views it years from now, it will remind him of the decision he made to accept Jesus Christ as his Savior and Lord.

Can you begin to sense the value in doing this? It reminds everyone of a commitment that was made. It implicitly demands re-evaluation, measuring progress against that commitment. Even as I write these words, my spirit is stirred by the fact that tomorrow marks my spiritual birthday. I find myself measuring my spiritual growth against my physical growth, all the while renewing the commitment I made many years ago.

Second, in attempting to mark and measure a child's spiritual growth, we would do well to learn from the Jewish practice of a Bar Mitzvah for a son or Bat Mitzvah for a daughter. The Hebrew terms mean "son of the commandment" or "daughter of the commandment." At a typical Bar or Bat Mitzvah, the young Jewish boy or girl is publicly recognized as an adult who must answer directly to God.

I plan to have a "Bar Jeshua"—son of the Savior—for my boy and a "Bat Jeshua"—daughter of the Savior—for my little girl. It will be a public commissioning, a rite of passage into adulthood. It will be a celebration, filled with challenges. I long to read to them the words: "Do not let this Book of the Law depart from your mouth; meditate on it day and night, so that you may be careful to do everything written in it. Then you will be prosperous and successful. Have I not commanded you? Be strong and courageous. Do not be terrified; do not be discouraged, for the LORD your God will be with you wherever you go" (Josh. 1:8–9).

Despite our chaotic and changing times, our children can be champions for Christ. But they need us to equip them for the battlefield by giving them the sword of the Spirit, which is the Word of God. And this involves us effectively communicating with our children. That's no small task!

GUIDELINES FOR TALKING ABOUT SEX

Linguists tell us there are over two thousand known languages in the world, not counting those spoken by teenagers!

I don't know whom to blame, but the reality is that most parents and teens are not communicating.

Teens seem to have their own vernacular, which many parents describe as being a guttural grunt. Ask a question, any question, and your teen grunts back an answer.

Each month popular author Judy Blume receives thousands of letters from young people looking for solutions to their deepest problems. They want help and for some reason cannot or will not turn to Mom or Dad. So they write to Judy.

Dear Judy,

What I wrote for is that I've got a problem. I just turned twelve and since then my mother and I haven't been so close. I don't see her all day. Then, when she comes home from work, she's so tired and ill I don't get to talk to her much.

We've always been so close and now this. I'm really scared and I don't know how to tell her or how to let my feelings out in the open. I hope you don't mind me asking you but I had no one else to turn to. My father wouldn't understand and I'd be embarrassed to say anything to him. Have you ever slowly been separated from someone you love?

Samantha, age 12[3]

Samantha's words could be found on the lips of many Christian young people. My parents are too busy to listen. My father won't understand. I am scared and I don't have anyone to talk to.

Can you and your adolescent or teenager sit down and talk together? Can you get beyond surface issues? If you want to teach your child how to walk in the truth, you must be able and willing to communicate. And that involves listening as well as talking. Communication is a two-way street. Try to make it run one way and you will end up alone, at a dead end.

Discussing sex will certainly put your relationship and your communication skills to the test. So make sure you implement the guidelines that follow.

Be Relaxed

Embarrassment creates anxiety. And anxiety usually cripples communication. If you get uncomfortable talking about sex, you will make your child feel uneasy, and the tension may very well destroy her openness.

When we get uptight, we communicate several negative messages. First of all, anxiety expresses uncertainty, a lack of knowledge. On a visit to the obstetrician several days before our first child was to be born, I asked the doctor several questions he struggled to answer. I got petrified thinking that this guy would deliver our baby. Anxiety can create the same kind of uncertainty with a child.

Our embarrassment can also be taken to mean that we have a negative outlook on sex. How else does the mind of a child understand our discomfort? If we are uncomfortable talking about sex, a child reasons there must be something wrong or threatening.

Next time the topic of sex enters a conversation, make sure you smile . . . even if your stomach growls, your blood pressure rises, or nausea begins to set in.

Be Positive

When we speak negatively about sex, we play into Satan's strategy. The media paints Christians as cosmic killjoys determined to destroy anything fun and enjoyable. When our young people accept this stereotype, we stand a good chance of losing them to the world. Who wants to team up with a band of cosmic killjoys?

Put yourself in your child's shoes for just a moment. From a thousand different angles you are bombarded with messages that communicate sex as the ultimate experience. Then you talk with your mom or dad and they imply sex is the ultimate evil. Whom are you going to believe, especially when you begin to have some strong sexual desires?

A positive presentation of sex that accurately reflects the truth of the Scriptures will cut the sorely needed path between liberty and legalism. Sex is a wonderful experience of intimacy that God reserved for marriage. A bold confidence in God's perfect plan for physical intimacy will explode the world's sexual stereotype of Christians and allow our young people to be proud of their faith.

Don't Overreact

A young boy blurted out, "You know something, Mom, I am really horny." This usually calm and collected mom became a gorilla and covered her son with a blanket of stern words. When she calmed down, the boy told her he really didn't know what "horny" meant. She then told him that his execution would be in order if he ever used that word (or any like it) again.

Whenever your child initiates a conversation about sex, remember: You want to encourage openness. You want him to come to *you,* not to someone else, with questions about sex. Also, understand that he may have brought the subject up to see how you'll respond. He may just want to see you come unglued. Finally, realize that he may be operating in ignorance and really needs your godly guidance. So take a deep breath; count to ten; then ask him to repeat his question. That will give you a chance to regain your composure. Later, you may even regain your sanity!

Accept Their Sexuality

Our children grow up faster than we ever imagine. Wasn't it just yesterday he was all nervous and excited about going to school? Now he's nervous and excited about the opposite sex. What happened? It's called puberty, and it occurs between the ages of ten and thirteen. Almost overnight a child's body changes. It's natural and expected but still unsettling for a child and parent alike.

Throughout these years of sexual development, parents need to be a rudder of acceptance. Don't ignore the obvious. If you inadvertently find your child masturbating, don't let your silence condemn him. If your son has a wet dream (nocturnal emission), explain what happened in a gentle, nonjudgmental way. When your daughter's breasts develop, tell her she is growing up to be a beautiful woman.

Whatever you do, don't joke about your child's sexuality. One misplaced word can cut deeply into your child's sensitive spirit.

Identify with Their Struggles

A number of parents have asked, "Should I share my past indiscretions with my children?" Identifying with a child's sexual battles does not mean we tell them the details of our past failures. Yes, they need to know that we have had to deal with many of the same problems and temptations they face. Yes, they need to know we have struggled in the past. But empathy does not require total openness. In fact, telling them too much might be damaging.

A Christian girl who allowed herself to be used sexually by a number of boys, when confronted about her behavior, commented that her parents "had to" get married. Desensitized by knowing her parents' sin, this confused teen felt the freedom to do whatever she wanted. Her parents' failure, rather than the Word of God, became the standard for her behavior.

We don't need to tell all. All we need to build mutual understanding is to share some common experiences in general terms. A boy who gets embarrassed having an erection welcomes reassurance from a dad who has been there. When thoughts of sex seem to dominate, a young person likes to know that someone else has felt the relentless tug of temptation. Identification builds integrity into our message. Empathy offers encouragement. The more we can relate to our children's experience, the greater our potential impact on their lives.

Take Advantage of Opportunities to Discuss Sex

Silence deafens. It gets so loud it can penetrate a person's heart. A father and son watch a condom commercial together, but neither says a word. An entire family watches a network special on AIDS, and no one says a word.

Initiating a conversation about sex expresses concern, openness, and availability. An open-ended question like "What do you think about _____?" can be a barometer of understanding or guilt. While blood pressure readings gauge physical health, our children's answers to our questions can gauge their spiritual and emotional health. Refusing to answer may indicate a relational problem or guilt. An obscure response usually points to ignorance or uncertainty.

Bridge a conversation out of concern for your teen, or take advantage of a given opportunity. If something appears to be wrong, take some time to probe—gently and lovingly, not like the Grand Inquisitor. The sooner you deal with the problem, the easier it will be to solve it.

Unashamedly Turn to the Scriptures

When my father tried to talk to me about sex, he became very frustrated. He told me I should treat girls I dated as if they were my own sisters. I asked him why. He didn't have a good answer. He told me sex was for married couples. Again, I asked him why. Still no good answer. If we had been Christians at the time, he would have had some answers based on the authority of God and His Word. He could have opened the Bible and shown me what God says. I might not have listened to him, but maybe I would have listened to God.

If our children are going to walk in the truth, they must learn to respond to the truth. That's why we need to turn, unashamedly and repeatedly, to the only God-inspired source of written truth—the Bible.

"But how do I do it? Where do I turn? What do I say?" The chapters ahead will give you some answers.

Express Your Unconditional Love

Their son came home from college with an earring in his left ear. They didn't know what to say. He had gotten away from the Lord. His appearance, attitudes, and actions revealed a rebellious heart. A message of unconditional love heard several weeks before still echoed in their minds. They both openly expressed their love for their son. No matter what he did, no matter how he dressed, they would love him.

Just days after he returned to school, they got a call from the dean of students, who wanted to know what had happened to their son. Since they didn't know what he was talking about, the dean told them that their son had removed his earring, trimmed his hair, changed his clothes, and recommitted his life to Christ. When asked about the dramatic change in his life, this young man said that his parents' love had reminded him that God loved him.

At times it will be difficult to face our child's sexual struggles while communicating God's love. But our expressions of concern must always be painted on a canvas of unconditional love and acceptance. We must offer words such as:

> *Son, I just want what's best for you, and I sincerely believe God's way is best. If you don't follow His plan, you can get hurt. I would hate to see you pay a terrible price for a bad decision. But no matter what you do, I will always love you.*

Listen When They Talk

Parents are notorious for ignoring their children. A wave of preoccupation prevails in many households, and strained relationships fall in its wake. You can't afford to let this happen. The cure lies in tuning in your teen and tuning out the world. That's what it takes to get beyond superficial conversation to real communication. Young children will pester us until they get our attention, but adolescents tend to walk away when they can't get us to focus. A father who had mastered the art of just playing along with his children's back-seat comments soon had his little boy grabbing his cheeks and saying, "Daddy, you are not listening!" Many teens probably wish they could do the same.

In listening to your child, be very observant and sensitive. Listen with your inner ear, noting nervousness, facial gestures, and general expressions. The emotional turmoil a growing number of young people face can be hidden by layers of confusion. Look beyond the surface. See the real struggles your child is having.

Maybe it's time to do relational by-pass surgery to restore the flow of communication between you and your child. Don't let anything block the lifeblood of your relationship. Let openness, sensitivity, love, and concern flow through your interaction. Create a nonthreatening atmosphere in which you can teach your child about God's good gift.

GIVE IT SOME THOUGHT

1. How would you define the goal of parenting?

2. Does your child love God? Has your child's love for God grown or diminished with age?

3. How can you mark your child's spiritual growth and important milestones?

4. On a scale from one to ten, with ten being the best, how would you rate your communication with your child? How can you improve it?

5. Does your child feel you accept his or her sexuality? Why or why not?

6. Are you relaxed and positive talking about sex?

7. What opportunities can you anticipate for turning to the Scriptures to teach your child about sex?

CHAPTER 6

God's Good Gift

My father-in-law happens to be a preacher, and one I greatly
admire. He has had a tremendous impact on my life
through his messages and even more so through his model.

When Teri and I decided to get married, he gave us his blessing
and agreed to perform the ceremony. In keeping with his usual
practice, we had to go through a series of counseling sessions. At
the first session he gave a relationship inventory that asked questions like, "How well do you get along with your future mother-in-
law?" The next question was the flip side: "How well do you get
along with your future father-in-law?" Talk about being put on the
spot.

While the inventory made me feel a bit uncomfortable, our final
session on sex made me squirm. How many men have had to hear
about sex from their fathers-in-law? We sat in a tight circle—
eyeball to eyeball. As we closed our eyes to pray, I had visions of a
father in anguish reluctantly placing his daughter on the altar of
sexual sacrifice—a modern rendition of Abraham and Isaac.

Five minutes into our session I discovered that God wasn't down
on sex and neither was my father-in-law. In fact, he said that the
Bible commands a married couple to enjoy one another freely and
to the fullest. I wish I had a tape of that session because it's a message many young people, not to mention their parents, need to hear.
They need to hear it because many of them have been sold a lie.

Since the first century, some Christians have held strange, scripturally unsound views of sex. In response to the Greek culture (that
encouraged sexual license because the body was unimportant)

came the ascetic view that demanded celibacy for effective service. The emphasis on celibacy created the belief that abstinence was a mark of spirituality. It wasn't until the Reformation, which began in the sixteenth century, that the church re-examined what the Bible had to say about sex. Unfortunately, the mistaken views of the early church still linger in some Christian circles, and they give our culture a field day making all Christians look like pathetic, pompous prudes.

Most Christian adults have no trouble handling the parody of Christianity and sex that pornographers perpetrate. But our young people—that's another story. In the tug of war over values, they are keenly aware of the world's disdain for Christian morality. Although based on lies and misrepresentation, the world's attack can nonetheless cause a child to question and doubt the biblical viewpoint.

Our children must understand that we are not against sex. Sex is wonderful and we want to enjoy it to the fullest. That's why we follow God's commands. As the Creator of sex, He is the best qualified to specify the boundaries of its expression for the greatest enjoyment of its benefits. Who are we to think otherwise? And yet, many self-proclaimed experts think they know more about sex than God does, and they call Christians prudes for thinking differently than they do. But Tottie Ellis responds to them in a way that exposes the real ignorance:

> Under the flag of realism, it has become fashionable to praise candidness in sex, to converse in four-letter-word frankness about the most basic functions of the body, and to favor total bluntness in speech on TV, in magazines, and in everyday conversation.
>
> Every attempt has been made to remove from our lives any semblance of decency and restraint. Today, "heaven knows, anything goes." What has gone is commitment, discipline, and making distinctions between right and wrong. What has come is the trivialization of sex and the refusal on the part of many to partake of relationships in depth. . . .
>
> The fact that most people in the USA do not want their moral sensibilities bombarded by indecencies does not mean we are opposed to sex or insensitive to sexually transmitted diseases. Quite the

contrary. It shows that we respect sex so much that we do not want to see it demeaned.

In the past two decades, sex has become de-sacrilized. This may look good in the short haul, but nature has written a book on the prescription of life that, in the long haul, a lack of standards always means disaster and death.[1]

We must prepare our children to stand up against the critics of biblical Christianity. And our children's best defense is a good offense—a proper presentation and modeling of biblical truth.

THE LORD IS FOR THE BODY

A biblical attitude toward sex begins with an appreciation for the body as the tool of sexual expression. Like the ancient ascetics, if we look at the body as evil, we will treat it as our enemy rather than as our ally.

The Bible's view of the human body challenges those that tend to devalue and even degrade it. God's Word says that by its very nature the body is good. Although it can be used in the wrong way, it is intrinsically good.

Handcrafted by God

When God finished creating the universe he took a step back and looked at it and "saw all that He had made, and it was very good" (Gen. 1:31). The climax of His creative work was the creation of Adam and his counterpart, Eve. Adam recognized the wonders of the divine craftsman when he looked upon Eve and shouted with delight,

> This is now bone of my bones
> and flesh of my flesh;
> she shall be called 'woman,'
> for she was taken out of man.   (Gen. 2:23)

The entrance of sin into the world did not destroy the basic goodness of the human body. Paul reminded the early church that although creation has come under the negative influence of sin, what God created remains good. "For *everything* God created is good, and nothing is to be rejected. . ." (1 Tim. 4:4, italics added). Since God created the human body and all that He created is good, the body, even with its needs and desires, is good.

Designed to Serve

Responding to the faulty beliefs of the Corinthians, the apostle Paul wrote, "The body is not meant for sexual immorality but for the Lord, and the Lord for the body" (1 Cor. 6:13). In other words, the Lord sees the body as good and does not want it used improperly. In Romans 6:13, Paul further contrasts the proper and improper uses of the body: "Do not offer the parts of your body to sin, as instruments of wickedness, but rather offer yourselves to God, as those who have been brought from death to life; and offer the parts of your body to him as instruments of righteousness."

Our bodies are tools to accomplish God's work in the world: "For we [living in our bodies] are God's workmanship, created in Christ Jesus to do good works, which God prepared in advance for us to do" (Eph. 2:10). One day we will give an account "for the things done while in the body, whether good or bad" (2 Cor. 5:10). Notice that the things done through the body can be good or bad, valuable or worthless. It's up to us. The body is our tool to glorify God. He gave it to us to serve Him. Therefore, it's not only good in itself, but it can also be used to do His good work.

Bought at a Price, Comes with a Promise

The death of Jesus Christ purchased us body, soul, and spirit. In 1 Corinthians 6:19–20, Paul refers to the body as our dwelling place which was purchased at Calvary. Our bodies were bought with Christ's death. And His resurrection guarantees that He will one day get all He paid for, including us in incorruptible, immortal bodies, even better bodies than we have now.

Would Jesus Christ give His life for something of little value? Would He bother to resurrect something that was worthless? No way! His death and resurrection make it clear that our bodies are important to God and should be important to us.

Does your child respect her body and view it as a gift from God? Or does she abuse it on the altar of instant gratification? If a young person adopts a biblical view of the body and a divine definition of sex, her perspective will promote lifelong purity.

Having considered God's view of the body, let's now look at His view of sex.

SEX—A DIVINE DEFINITION

What is sex? To the prostitute, it's a commodity to be sold. To the media merchants, it's a sure way to attract an audience. To most, it's the ultimate passion and pleasure.

How would you define sex? What words come to your mind? Do you focus on the physical act, or do you think of a relationship? Does your definition reflect a positive perspective or a painful past? How do you think your child would define sex? Would sex be associated with dating, love, and romance? Would he view sex as the pleasure passage to adulthood? Our definition of sex determines our attitude toward it, which in turn directs our actions. If we define sex as a commodity, we will sell it. If we define it as an attention getter, we will flaunt it. If it's the ultimate passion and pleasure, we will pursue it at any cost to ourselves or others. If we define it as a gift from God, we will respect and genuinely enjoy it.

Defining sex in the twentieth century is no easy task. Our society has abandoned the Judeo-Christian ethic as archaic. Now millions of people look to moral midgets, self-proclaimed experts who sell sex for a living. These purveyors of pornography invade our homes under the guise of First Amendment rights. Dismissing parental authority, they demand access to our phone lines, television sets, and video libraries to seek out a growing market of minors.

It's time for hedonism to end. It's time to return to a biblical view of sex. For the Christian there is no other choice. The spiritual dimension must serve as a rudder that directs our minds as well as our actions. So let's turn to God's Word and see what it says about sex, and let's see how we can explain it to our children.

According to the Scriptures,

**Sex is God's good gift to a married couple
for their enjoyment and for having children.**

Sex is a wedding present filled with delights that last a lifetime. It's communion between a couple that can produce another person. It's a sacred union made possible by divine design.

Sex Is God's Idea

When it comes to sex, God is its author, creator, and designer. It's His invention. He built the first prototype and made sure it worked just the way it should. But in the milleniums that have passed, many people have come along and sold cheap imitations. But the original is still available, and it has not been lost or improved upon. It's the original that we as parents need to sell to our children.

God's patent on sex cannot be found in Washington, D.C., but it can be studied in the book of Genesis. There we read that when God created people, He gave them bodies that complemented each other: "Male and female he created them" (Gen. 1:27). He could have created a single-sex species that reproduced itself. In fact, when you look at creation, you can see other forms of life that reproduce without sexual union. But God didn't choose to make us that way. Instead, He created a man and a woman to join their flesh perfectly in a face-to-face oneness that defies comparison.

Does your child appreciate the significance of God being the creator of sex? Does your child understand that God's Word is the owner's manual from the one who made us sexual beings? Does he or she see God as the author of physical intimacy? Here's how I would communicate this to a young person:

> *If you had trouble writing a program for your computer, to whom would you turn for help? Would you ask me for help? Probably not, since I don't know a thing about computers. Would you ask a friend who tried to write the same program but failed?*
>
> *What if you could talk to the person who made the computer, created the computer's language, and wrote a program like the one you're working on? Would you expect him to have the answers?*
>
> *Apply this same line of thinking to sex. Who made it? Who designed it? God did, and since He did, it makes sense that if we want to make it be all it can be, we should look to Him as the primary source of information.*

Sex Is Good

Some parents hesitate to tell their children that sex is good. They fear their words will tempt their child. But there's nothing a parent can say that will tempt a child more than what he sees on television, walking through a mall, or listening to his friends. Of course, communicating sex as good does not mean we offer seductive details, rather it's presenting sex truthfully and placing it in its proper context.

Be very careful not to communicate a negative impression of sex. Some people's sexual experience has been warped by their parents' negativism. While the letter that follows is admittedly extreme, it illustrates my point.

From the time I was a tiny child, my mother often warned me, "Never let anyone see your body—not anyone—under any circumstances." One day, when I was six years old and my brother was eight, my parents left us on the farm while they drove to a town some distance away to get some groceries. Toward the end of the two hours, my brother began to plead with me to let him see my body and he would let me see him. After resisting for a while I finally gave in to his urging. We stood about eight feet apart as stiff as wooden soldiers. Then we dressed quickly in case our parents should drive up. When my mother noticed I was very quiet and depressed, she questioned me, and I told her the whole story. My father beat my brother with a heavy leather belt making great red welts and bruises on his legs. I could hear him screaming from behind the barn. I thought my father would never stop lashing him.

I felt so sad I lay down on my bed and cried in my pillow. My mother came in to talk to me. She was very angry, but I believe she was telling me what she believed. She said that men and women who took their clothes off and forgot all about trying to be good were the worst kind of sinners in God's sight—and this was the unpardonable sin God would never forgive. She said my brother and I had come close to committing this sin and it might be a long time before God would forgive and love us again. She told me that if a man and a woman were married, it was still wrong unless they wanted to have a baby.

This dear woman now realizes that her parents had a grossly distorted, unbiblical view of marital love. But because she lived with her parents' perspective for so long, she still, as a married woman, has deep feelings of guilt after intercourse with her husband.

On the positive side, I know a man with three daughters who openly presented sex to them as a gift from God. Whenever he talked about sex, he did so in a wholesome and discreet way. A week before his oldest daughter's wedding, he took her out for dinner and encouraged her to experience freely the magnificence of marital love. He knew that she already believed sex was good, and he wanted her to enjoy it thoroughly within God's designated boundaries.

Do you want your child to enjoy sex with his or her spouse? God does. So should you. As married adults, your children will reap sexual fulfillment from the seeds you plant in the early years of their lives.

Sex Is a Gift

God's Word treats sex as a gift that accompanies marriage. Comparing singleness with marriage, Paul wrote, "Each man has his own gift from God; one has this gift, another has that" (1 Cor. 7:7). Some receive the gift of marriage and sexual union while others receive the gift of singleness and celibacy.

Impressing upon our children that sex is a gift has several advantages. When you call it a gift you make a positive statement. It's a gift, not a curse. A gift is something given, not taken. To take a gift before it has been given robs the giver. We use gifts to make special occasions. As such, the wedding night is marked by unwrapping the gift of union and consummating the relationship sexually.

Out of the personal experience of your family you can find some examples that teach this important concept. Here's how I would explain this to my adolescent son:

> *Do you remember years ago when you wanted a skateboard and I kept telling you to wait until you were older and could handle it? When Mom found one on sale, she bought it, planning to save it for your next birthday. When you saw the box, you decided you didn't*

*want to wait so you went and opened it. It wasn't fifteen minutes
before you almost broke your arm.*

*God treats sex as a gift He wants to give you when you are ready
to enjoy and appreciate it without the fear of getting hurt. That's why
He wants you to wait until you are married to open His gift.*

Sex Is for Marriage

How do you know the gift of sex is just for marriage? As a new
believer I asked that question of several Christians who could not
give me an answer. They told me that's what God said and they were
vehement advocates of their position, but they could not show me
from the Bible that it was true.

Our children will ask us the same question. Where does God say
that sex is to be reserved for marriage? Are you ready with an answer? If not, read on and let me suggest a way to respond.

Although there are relevant passages in the Old Testament, to
simplify your explanation, I would concentrate on the Greek
term *porneia,* which is found in the New Testament. *Porneia* refers
to all sexual activities outside of marriage—premarital, extramarital, homosexual, and the like. The term is translated into English as
fornication or immorality.

At times the context of a given passage defines the term more
specifically. For example, in 1 Corinthians 5:1 *porneia* refers to
incest: "It is actually reported that there is sexual immorality
among you, and of a kind that does not occur even among pagans: A
man has his father's wife." In Romans 1:29 the context indicates
that *porneia* refers to homosexual activity. Usually, however, the
term covers all forms of sexual activity outside of marriage, as is
indicated in 1 Corinthians 7:2: "But since there is so much immorality *(porneia)* each man should have his own wife, and each
woman her own husband."

The only corrective for sexual immorality is sex between a man
and a women in marriage. Paul noted this centuries ago: "Now to
the unmarried and the widows I say: It is good for them to stay
unmarried, as I am. But if they cannot control themselves, they
should marry, for it is better to marry than to burn with passion"
(1 Cor. 7:8–9). Premarital and extramarital sex is wrong. Working

through this passage with teens I like to emphasize the obvious. "God's provision for your passion," I say, "is not your girlfriend or boyfriend. It is a husband or a wife."

A distraught mother called me concerned about her daughter and the young man she was dating. The night before, the couple had had a fight, and this guy put his fist through the wall. He agreed to meet with me to discuss what happened. After about twenty minutes of listening to inane excuses, I asked him if he and this girl were sexually involved. His face told me yes while his words said no. Then I asked him if I could give it to him straight. I said, "You lost your temper because the two of you have been going to bed, but now you want out of the relationship and she feels used, right?" If he had worn dentures, they would have dropped in his lap. Then I said, "If you are serious about your relationship with Jesus Christ, you should either stop having sex or marry the girl so you can have sex whenever you want. Are you ready to get married?" He quickly responded, "No." I came back just as quickly, "Then cut it out."

That's what I tell teens. If you think you are ready to have sex, you also have to be ready to get married—unless you want to tell God that you don't care what He says.

Another important passage is Hebrews 13:4, which tells us, "Marriage should be honored by all, and the marriage bed kept pure, for God will judge the adulterer and all the sexually immoral." If married people have sex outside of their relationship, they are involved in adultery. If unmarried people have sex, they are committing fornication. We can only honor the marriage bed by keeping it pure, and we keep it pure by not allowing anyone outside the marriage to invade the bed.

If, after you go over these passages with your child, she is still not convinced God condemns premarital sex, do a study of virginity. Virginity was held in such high regard in Bible days that it had to be proven on the wedding night. When the groom came to pick up his bride, he would bring her to his home and would consummate their relationship. If his bride was a virgin, the thin membrane over the vagina would be broken through intercourse and a small spot of blood would be found on the bedcloth. That cloth was given to the father of the bride so he could always show that his daughter was a virgin when she got married (Deut. 22:13–19). If a new bride could not substantiate her virginity, she could be stoned to death (Deut. 22:20, 21).

The character of God has not changed since He commanded that sexual sin be purged from Israel. He still hates sexual sin. We should not presume that because He is gracious and no longer requires that fornicators be stoned, He has changed His mind about this act. On the contrary, He cannot alter His standard of holiness because it is grounded in His unchangeable nature (Mal. 3:6, 1 Pet. 1:14–16). Sexual sin remains a very serious matter for parent and child alike.

Sex Is for Pleasure

Pure pleasure is one of the primary reasons God created sex. Tragically, some Christians never come to comprehend this fact. One of the first letters we received in our office came from a seventy-nine-year-old woman who had heard a message entitled "God's Purpose for Sex." Her letter dripped with emotion as she told of being married for fifty-five years, all the while believing that God intended sex only as a vehicle for having children. She described how she resisted her husband's advances. Now she recognized her wrong, but it was too late. Her husband had died several years before, and now she had to live with deep regrets.

Rather than regrets, let's experience scriptural reality. Throughout the Old Testament we find examples and statements of the pleasurable aspects of sex. In Genesis 26:8, Isaac and Rebekah are seen "caressing" or petting or, as another translation says, "sporting." No matter how you translate the term, it carries with it the idea of mutual pleasure.

Whenever I meet a non-Christian who believes that God hates sex, I like to turn to Deuteronomy 24:5 where we find a fascinating command: "If a man has recently married, he must not be sent to war or have any other duty laid on him. For one year he is to be free at home and bring happiness to the wife he has married." Now a husband was to bring happiness to his wife in a number of ways, but at the top of the list was sexual pleasure. If you don't believe me, just ask any newlyweds what they plan to do on their honeymoon.

Many passages teach the pleasurable purpose of sex, and one of the most direct statements can be found in the wisdom literature called Proverbs:

> May your fountain be blessed,
> and may you rejoice in the wife of your youth.
> A loving doe, a graceful deer—
> may her breasts satisfy you always,
> may you ever be captivated by her love.
>   (Prov. 5:18–19)

Verse 18 tells the wise man to "rejoice" in the wife he married when he was young. Then verse 19 defines how he can rejoice: Let her breasts satisfy you, let her love captivate you. The wise sage is saying that God wants a husband and wife to be exhilarated by their physical union. Note the emphasis is on pleasure, not procreation.

If you remain unconvinced, turn to the Song of Solomon and study it as a biblical guide for married love. The entire book describes the bedroom bliss of Solomon and his bride. Here's one small section:

> I belong to my lover, and his desire is for me.
> Come, my lover, let us go to the countryside,
> let us spend the night in the villages.
> Let us go early to the vineyards to see if the vines have budded,
> if their blossoms have opened, and if the pomegranates are in
>   bloom—
> there I will give you my love.   (Song of Sol. 7:10–12)

Ample evidence from the Old Testament supports the pleasurable purpose of sex. The New Testament simply adds additional weight. In the New Testament, mutual sexual satisfaction and enjoyment are commanded by God: "The husband should fulfill his marital duty to his wife, and likewise the wife to her husband" (1 Cor. 7:3). What's that "duty"? The duty is to provide pleasure in response to passion.

At this point you may wonder if you should teach your child that God designed sex to be pleasurable. Absolutely. Ignorance of the pleasurable aspects of sex won't keep a young person pure, especially when our world worships at the altar of sexual pleasure. Friends or the media will tell our teens about sexual pleasure. They *will* hear about it. The only question is, will they hear about it from them or from us? They need to hear us tell them what the Word of God says, and they need to hear that God has designed sex for pleasure within the confines of marriage.

Sex is for Having Children

One of the Creator's first commands was "Be fruitful and increase in number; fill the earth and subdue it" (Gen. 1:28). How? "A man will leave his father and mother and be united to his wife, and they will become one flesh" (Gen. 2:24).

The obvious connection between sex and pregnancy cannot be overstated to our youth. Pleasure and procreation both come under the umbrella of responsibility. While sexual pleasure can be experienced apart from having children, entering into the union demands a willingness to accept the potential product of that union. In other words, if you want to have the pleasure, you must also be willing to accept the product. That product may well be another person—a baby. Impress upon your teenager that one cannot have the first gift unless one is willing to accept the second. If you are ready to have sex, then you must be willing to get married and accept the responsibility for raising the product of your union. You cannot depend on contraceptives; they are not foolproof. And abortion is an unacceptable form of birth control.

Sex is God's good gift to a married couple for their pleasure and for having children. This simple definition summarizes much of what God says about sex. Young people who understand and accept this definition will have their sexual identity indelibly marked by biblical truth designed to bring joy and marital fulfillment.

But many young people will spurn what God says about sex. What should you do then? In the next chapter, I will discuss how to use the practical aspects of the Bible to reach the resistant child.

GIVE IT SOME THOUGHT

1. How would your child define sex?

2. How might your child's definition influence his or her sexual behavior?

3. Do your words and actions communicate a positive or negative view of sex?

4. Does your child appreciate God's authorship of sex? Is your child willing to look to God as the divine designer of our sexuality?

5. Does your child understand and accept that sex outside of marriage is wrong?

6. What opportunities can you anticipate to communicate a biblical definition of sex to your child?

CHAPTER 7

The Wisdom of Waiting

We live in the age of the quick fix. If you want it, get it, the sooner the better.

Just the other day I saw a woman lose her temper after missing an open section of a revolving door. Minutes later a man blew his cork because he had to wait too long at a fast-food drive-in window. Rumor has it that a severe "Mac Attack" can do that to you.

Visit the Nieder household on a Sunday night, and you will see the quick fix in high gear around 8:00 P.M. That's when the demon of Dunkin' Donuts strikes. Despite diet or debt, our household regularly surrenders to the overwhelming desire for any and all varieties of donut delights. With coupon in hand, I get in the car, set it on autopilot, then sit back and salivate. When I get home Teri interrogates me: "How many are left?" The next question seems inevitable: "How many did you get?" As a gifted graduate of Wheaton College, she then subtracts and begins to preach her favorite message on gluttony.

In countless ways, we can see that our society has discarded the discipline of waiting. Adults and children alike seldom learn to forgo immediate gratification of their desires. In fact, our desires tend to direct us rather than our directing them. How does instant gratification influence our children, especially when they get the "urge to merge"?

Our young people don't want to wait for anything. In many ways we have taught them to be tyrannized by their desires, to demand satisfaction, right now and at any price.

Our easy-credit and fast-food curriculum has graduated thousands of young people who, when confronted with biblical morality, ask, "Why wait until marriage to have sex? I don't wait for anything else."

The studies I cited earlier show most Christian young people will not wait. Why? There are a number of reasons, but they all boil down to one: Christian youth really don't care that God commands them to wait. They have rejected His authority. They have decided to do what *they* want, not what *He* wants.

How should we respond to this spiritual crisis? We must challenge the spiritually mature to a greater depth of commitment and the immature to a new or more consistent commitment. Even a young person who refuses to obey God needs to understand that God's commands are in his or her best interest.

We begin with God no matter what our child's spiritual condition. We can argue all the practical reasons to wait, but it's their relationship with God that will bring about significant, lifelong change in their attitudes and actions. Foremost in our thinking must be our child's spiritual growth and development, which is a product of obedience.

WAITING IS AN ACT OF OBEDIENCE

Obedience has become a rare commodity in our day. Champions of individual rights raise their banners in the name of freedom, but they frequently do so at the expense of authority. Just ask any employer. You will hear story after story of individuals who could not accept authority.

If I could teach my children one thing, it would be to obey God. If they learn to obey God, they will agree to obey me because that is what God commands (Eph. 6:1)! If they learn to obey God, they will live a pure life because that's what God commands (1 Thess. 4:3). Obeying God is the catalyst for Christian living for children and parents alike.

Why should a young person wait until marriage in order to have sex? The first and most important answer is that God says to wait:

It is God's will that you should be sanctified: that you should avoid sexual immorality; that each of you should learn to control his own body in a way that is holy and honorable, not in passionate lust like the heathen, who do not know God; and that in this matter no one should wrong his brother or take advantage of him. The Lord will punish men for all such sins, as we have already told you and warned you. For God did not call us to be impure, but to live a holy life. Therefore, he who rejects this instruction does not reject man but God, who gives you his Holy Spirit (1 Thess. 4:3–8).

Note the phrase "It is God's will" and also "He who rejects this instruction does not reject man but God." God's will and God's instruction permeate every aspect of this passage. His command is "Wait!" No one else's instruction or opinion really matters.

So when you share this passage with your child, be sure to emphasize obedience. Here's one way to do that:

> *Son, it took me a long time to learn that the best thing I could do was to obey God. If there is one thing in life I want to encourage you to do, it is to obey God also.*
>
> *In this passage the Lord has told us what He wants. He wants us to avoid sexual immorality. That means I am to have a sexual relationship with only your mom, no other person. The passage also means that you cannot have a sexual relationship until you are married. If we turn our backs on this teaching, we will not only hurt ourselves but others in our family and God as well.*

Another way to encourage obedience is to compare God's law with man's. For example, why is there a law that says a teenager cannot drive until the age of sixteen? Aren't some teens capable of driving at an earlier age? And aren't there some benefits to being able to drive sooner?

But despite some obvious benefits, the law still stands: a young person cannot get a license to drive before a certain age. A person who breaks this law pays the price—a fine, a stay in jail, a revoked license, or perhaps even a serious injury or death.

The law is not there to ruin anyone's fun. It exists to protect us and others who drive. We may not like what it says or agree with the reasons for its enactment, but it's on the books, and it will be enforced.

Now think of God's law. A child is capable of having sex before marriage, but God's law says no. Some people feel there are benefits to having sex before marriage, but the law says no. We may see no need for this command, but someone far wiser than we established it. It was established not to ruin our fun, but to protect us and those around us.

Just as our society demands that we have a license to drive, so God demands that we have a license to love someone sexually. Neither our society nor God cares whether or not we like the law. What matters is that we obey it. And when we obey it, we will soon find that God's law exists because of His love for us (Jer. 7:23).

IT'S THE BEST THING FOR YOU

Regardless of God's love, however, many young people are in spiritual rebellion. They don't seem to care about honoring the Lord. So how should we respond to a child who acts like a rebel? We should continue to challenge him spiritually by explaining that God still loves him and that obeying God is in his best interest. In these ways, we will help move our child from immaturity to maturity, from thinking of himself as the master of his sexuality to realizing that God is. Tragically, it may take years of heartache before a rebellious child learns these lessons. But one day he may come to appreciate that God's commands grow out of God's love. When He says to wait until marriage to have sex, He has our well-being in mind.

Waiting Protects Your Self-Respect

My friend, Joe White of Kanakkuk Camps, shared with me a letter from a girl who allowed herself to be used as a sexual object and lost her self-respect in the process:

> I was at a party two years ago and I really liked this guy. Everyone had been drinking, including me. I was doing everything to let this guy know that I was alive. So he told me that he really liked me. He wanted to go all the way with me but I wouldn't let him. Then he would make out with me and do some things and run off with someone else to get something off of them. I still kept trying to get him to notice me. And again he would come back to me and then to someone else. Soon finally, everyone had gone from the party and he started pushing me again. Finally, I gave in. I felt like trash. He got

what he wanted, leading me to believe that he liked me. But he never did.

It disturbs me that a young, Christian girl could be so vulnerable. Sex became a form of recreation and a barometer of acceptance. Think of the years it may take for this girl to recover her self-respect. If she only had waited, her self-esteem could have remained intact.

You might read that girl's letter to your daughter and follow up with a comment such as this:

> *Sweetheart, I love you and God loves you. It is because we love you that we don't want to see you get hurt. If you have sex before you get married, you have a good chance of walking away feeling used and stripped of your dignity. In sex you give yourself away to the other person. If that person then walks away from you, you will feel cheap and used. You will have a deep sense of loss when you suddenly discover he wanted your body but not you.*

If you have a teen-age son, your exhortation would be different but just as direct.

> *Son, one big reason God tells you to wait until marriage to have sex is because he doesn't want you or any girl getting hurt by your relationship. If you have sex with a girl before marriage, you are going to take from her something that does not belong to you. You may rob her of her dignity, and she will walk away feeling cheap and used. No matter how many other guys she has been with, you will add to her lack of self-respect. God doesn't want you to go through life thinking about the heartache and pain you have caused some girl.*

Waiting Guarantees Freedom from Guilt

I used to think the biggest reason parents didn't talk to their children about sex was embarrassment. Now I believe it's the parents' lingering guilt over their own sexual failures—guilt our children can avoid by deciding to wait.

To make this point with your child recall a time in your child's life when he or she felt the pangs of guilt following personal failure.

Remind your child of the incident, touching the emotional threads of the past. Then draw an analogy. If you do this with your daughter, you might approach the subject this way:

> *Sweetheart, remember what happened when Jennifer overheard you say some negative things about her to the other girls at church? You knew she found out and it made you feel very uncomfortable. It took you days to apologize. And even after you apologized, whenever you saw Jennifer you wanted to crawl in a hole and hide. You just couldn't get over the guilt you felt.*
>
> *If you have sex with a boy, you will have some of the same feelings—only they will be much worse. Every time you see him you will feel uncomfortable. Even if you ask God to forgive you, you will still have a difficult time forgiving yourself. And when the relationship ends, your guilt will seem unbearable. The Lord doesn't want you to have to experience such heartache. That's why He wants you to wait until you are married to have a sexual relationship.*

Waiting Allows You to Build Relationships

"John, I don't know what is wrong with my son. He doesn't want to talk to us; doesn't care about church, school, or anything else. His mother is fit to be tied, and I can't figure out what's going on."

I asked if anything new had occurred in this boy's life. His dad pondered a moment and said, "Oh, yeah, he has a new girlfriend. I have only seen her once, but I think she's bad news."

I asked the obvious, "What do you mean, bad news?"

"Well, she looks like a-a-a prostitute."

I told him what I thought was happening, and several weeks later he confirmed my suspicions. This fifteen-year-old boy had lost his virginity. As a consequence, he became so consumed by sex that he was about to lose his mind to his passions.

When sex begins, a young couple's personal, I-Thou relationship typically ends. Sexual energies are so strong they tend to dominate once they are allowed to flourish. Physical intimacy quickly becomes an obstacle to relational intimacy—intimacy that brings emotional, spiritual, and intellectual oneness. They merge their bodies—nothing else.

The interplay between physical and relational intimacy differs for men and women, boys and girls. Boys will accept a relationship in order to get sex. Girls will give sex in order to have a relationship. This dynamic gives rise to the popular ploy used by young men to gain sexual access. It's the man who says, "If you love me (relationship) you'll have sex with me." Have you ever heard of a girl using the same line on a boy? Not likely. But this line seduces many young girls who will give away their bodies to satisfy their craving for an interpersonal relationship.

Our daughters need to be on their emotional guard, and we can help them by sounding the warning:

> *Sweetheart, God designed you to long for relationships. He has made you a caring and compassionate person. When you enter into a relationship with a young man, he will probably want sex to be included. If you allow sex to enter the picture, it will dominate his thinking and eventually yours. When that happens, it won't take long before the relational depth you want will be lost. Sex will not keep you together; it will drive you apart.*

Waiting Is a Safeguard Against Disease

He was big, strong, athletically gifted, but on this day he was an emotional wreck. Terror darted from his eyes as he tried to tell me what was happening. He had just returned from the health clinic. There the doctor wanted him to go the local hospital to confirm his diagnosis—venereal disease.

Fortunately, the physicians at the clinic contained my friend's disease with antibiotics, but he experienced a great deal of discomfort and pain and had to list his sexual liaisons to warn his previous partners.

The response to the growing epidemic of veneral disease and AIDS has been fascinating. Doctors, lawyers, and sociologists have suddenly come to the conclusion that God's way really is the best way. Terms such as abstinence and monogamy, once treated as archaic, have returned to our modern day vocabulary. Now the whole world is learning once again that purity protects. God's Word told us a long time ago. We just didn't want to listen.

We now have the choice opportunity to tell people God's law reflects God's love and to present it to our children this way:

*The Lord loves you so much He wants to protect you from getting a
sexual disease that will kill you. He knows that if you have sex just
one time with the wrong person, you may die from it. He also knows
that when you have sex with a person, you are biologically having
sex with everyone that person has had sex with before you! But if you
wait until you get married, you and your mate can have sex five times
a day with no fear of disease. Fatigue, yes. Disease, no.*

Waiting Preserves Your Future

Despite the widespread availability of contraceptives, teen pregnancy remains at an all-time high. Children are having children at
an alarming rate.

Over the years my wife and I have helped a number of courageous single, pregnant women put their babies up for adoption. But
despite their courage, all these women paid a tremendous price for
getting pregnant out of wedlock. For nine long months, they put
their lives on hold. Relationships with parents and some friends
became strained. Some even broke permanently. Typically, the men
who fathered the children were aloof, unsupportive, and at times
even abusive. The price of premarital sex was extremely high. One
teen has expressed the cost in a poetical lament:

> The new morality—and freedom.
> From classes—what a drag!
> From homework—senseless hours.
> From disciplines—useless.
> From church—a bore.
> I'm my own woman now.
> Made so by one decision,
> One hour of love and pleasure.
> Free now to look at my cheerleader sweater hanging in the closet.
> My books and baseball schedule resting on the shelf.
> My material from a prom formal, never made, as it sits amid the
> remnants of the fabrics left over from my maternity tops.
> My medals from band and choir, forsaken in the clutter of a jew-
> elry box.
> My friends passing by my window.
> Laughing over the gossip column in the school newspaper
> And giggling over who will be the next to experience

The new morality—and freedom!
From cleaning—what a drag!
From him—always arguing.
From ironing—senseless hours.
From dishes—useless.
From cooking—a bore.
From sex—a hang-up.
Oh, God, if you are there,
Please let someone take this crying baby off my hands.
And let my feet dance once more.
I am so old.
And I was never young.[1]

What a sad slice of reality. Premature intimacy comes with an expensive price tag. We must let young people count the cost before it's too late.

Here is one way to warn your daughter:

> *A sexual relationship carries with it a great degree of responsibility. You are responsible to God, to the person you are involved with, and to the person the two of you may bring into existence. The Lord knows you are not ready for that much responsibility, so He says wait. Wait until you have a man committed to you for life. Wait until you have a husband who will be your partner in the parenting task.*

Waiting Demonstrates Your Love for Others

One of the biggest problems of our generation is its preoccupation with self. We are self-centered people. We look out for number one. We do it our way without regard for anyone else. To counter this "me" mentality young people must realize how their behavior influences others. Their sexual conduct has a profound impact on a number of people other than themselves.

Waiting Shows Your Love for the Unborn

She had left him again, and in his loneliness, he asked me to come over to talk. Mark and Donna had been together two years, but now it was over. At first I felt sorry for this emotionally beaten man crushed by the weight of his wife's departure.

With tears in his eyes, he handed me letters Donna had sent him after their last breakup. I glanced down at one letter and saw it was signed not Donna but Skip. I went to the top of the page and read, "Dear Daddy, why did you kill me? We could be having so much fun together." As I asked Mark about the letter, another caught my eye: "Daddy, I would be over a year old now. I sure miss you. Love, Skip." Mark was sobbing, but he managed to squeeze out a brief explanation.

"Shortly after we met, Donna got pregnant. We didn't have enough money to get married and raise a child. So I had her get an abortion."

Now tears filled my eyes as I realized Skip was the name of the child Mark wouldn't allow to see daylight.

One of the most difficult decisions a young woman can ever face is whether to carry a baby to full term or have an abortion. Today abortion is held up as a quick fix for freedom. But is it? Just ask the woman who wrote:

> As a teen, I thought that sex was "okay" for any two people who were truly in love. I justified my sexual relationship to God by saying that, in a sense, my boyfriend and I were "really married" because we knew only each other. The end result of my sin was two unwanted pregnancies and eventually two abortions before I was 17. My family still doesn't know, and although I have received God's forgiveness, six years later I still grieve for those babies and wish I had waited until marriage.

Several years ago a young, unmarried couple came to me for counsel after they discovered she was pregnant. They wanted to know how God felt about abortion. I told them it was not an option. I explained that if God didn't want the baby to be born, He would make that choice, but it wasn't ours to make. Years later I received this letter:

> For quite some time I have been wanting to write you a letter. I want to thank you for taking time to counsel us. Your words of wisdom were much needed. You prevented us from adding to our sin and adding to our guilt. I shall never forget one thing you said—"If God

doesn't want the baby to live, He will take care of that Himself." I praise God that we listened. When I sit and ponder what has taken place in my life, I am so amazed. I am not amazed at God, but at the fact that He has taken my sin (our sin) and forgiven me. It took me almost a year to recover from my guilt. When I get "down" about it, I always remember that God has forgiven me and I count my blessings.

God did take their baby through a miscarriage. But the child was not the only product of their sin. Guilt over their illicit sexual union also hung over their lives. But they both realized that their guilt wasn't as great as the guilt they would have experienced from murdering their baby.

An unwanted pregnancy will tempt a young couple to destroy the innocent to cover their sin. But waiting eliminates the temptation.

You can explain the dilemma of an unwanted pregnancy to your child this way:

> *God says to wait until marriage because He doesn't want you to have to decide between yourself and the life of a baby that your body has brought into existence. If you get pregnant (get a girl pregnant), you may be tempted to murder an innocent person. God doesn't want you to commit one sin after another, trying to run from what you have done. If you wait until marriage, a baby will be a blessing, not a burden.*

Waiting Demonstrates Love for the Other Person

My parents didn't say much about sex, good, bad, or otherwise. As I mentioned before the one conversation I can remember with my dad took place when I was about seventeen and had a sister who was just two years old. He said to me, "John, when you go out with a girl, you ought to treat her like you would want someone to treat your sister." When he said this, I rolled my eyes up into my head and thought to myself, "Who would want to date a two-year-old anyway?"

But my father had a good point. If our teens are really concerned about the other person, then they will put premarital sex on hold. Just ask the typical teenage boy if he wants to marry a virgin or some girl who has slept around. Most will want a virgin. Those who suggest otherwise are lying. But then ask them, "Are you treating girls the way you want your future wife to be treated?" I guarantee you, that will be a new and staggering thought to them.

A father made this point in a conversation with his son who was about to go on a date. "Son, do you think you are going to marry the girl you're going out with tonight?"

"Well, no, Dad, I doubt it."

"Okay, son, I agree; but let me ask you another question. Do you think the girl you are going to one day marry might also be going out tonight with another guy?"

"Dad, I guess she might be."

"All right, son, how do you want this other guy to treat her?"

"Dad, if he touches her I will kill him!"

"I can understand how you feel, but let me ask you one more question. Do you think the girl you are going out with tonight will get married someday?"

"Yeah, probably."

"Then how do you think her future husband wants you to treat her?"

This father's point cuts to the core of the biblical admonition that in regard to sexual immorality, "No one should wrong his brother or take advantage of him" (1 Thess. 4:6). You could summarize this point for your son by emphasizing the essence of true love:

> *If you really love a girl, you will only do what's best for her. Premarital sex pulls her away from God, it cuts into her self respect, it undermines your relationship with her, and it can literally destroy her—as well as your—future happiness. If you really care about her, you will not take advantage of her for your own pleasure.*

Waiting Honors Your Parents

Children should not live for their parents but for their Lord. And if they live for Him, they will have a real sensitivity to their parents. Needless to say, we never threaten our children with losing our affection, but there is nothing wrong with telling them in advance the heartache we will share in their wrong choices.

If our children could hear others tell what it was like to confess their sins to mom and dad, the thought would deter premarital sex. I have had adults who, in remembering the experience, still break down uncontrollably.

Encouraging our children to honor us by their actions is biblical and can have a profound impact on their behavior. Senator Daniel Inouye of Hawaii is just one man who can testify to this fact. When he was eighteen and leaving home for the service, his father told him, "Whatever you do, do not dishonor the family." Inouye took his father's words to heart. During the Second World War, he was decorated for his courage in combat. He was awarded the Distinguished Service Cross and the Bronze Star. Since then he has spent more than thirty years of his life serving his country in Congress. Our children may not get the recognition of an Inouye, but by honoring us they will certainly receive the recognition of the Lord of the universe. That's no small honor!

Waiting Honors Your Future Spouse

It sent a chill up my spine when I found out my wife, Teri, had prayed for me before we even met. As she prayed, the Lord worked in my life in many miraculous ways to make it possible for Teri to have a Christian husband. But not only did she pray for me. She didn't bring any immoral baggage to our marriage; she kept herself for me. I want so much for my son to have the same kind of wife, and I want my daughter to be that kind of wife.

Premarital sex can undermine marital sex, and young people can grasp the problems that may carry over into marriage, including:

- Jealousy over past involvements;
- Comparing your spouse to previous partners;
- Feeling compared to previous partners.

The emotional and relational baggage of past involvement makes waiting the right thing to do.

THE CHALLENGE

Seize every opportunity to teach your child that because God loves her, He wants her to wait to have sex. Look for creative ways to repeat and reinforce your explanations to make sure your child understands the wisdom of this instruction. Don't be afraid to ask, "Do you plan to obey God and wait until you are married to have sex?" A very long moment of silence might follow. But don't say a word; just wait for an answer. If your child fails to respond or does so reluctantly, then gently probe, "Why are you uncomfortable?" Again, wait for an answer.

As you read your child's body language, you may want to become even more direct: "Are you having sex with someone or have you been sexually involved before? Do you need to talk about it?" In an atmosphere of love and acceptance, your child may very well open up. If not, pray some more and create the opportunity to talk again.

If your child opens up and admits to sexual involvement, do your best to pour on the love and concern. She knows she has done wrong. After the emotions settle, open up the Bible and show her that God forgives her as she confesses her sin (1 John 1:9). Then, calmly and nonjudgmentally, begin to work through the concepts presented throughout this book to avoid another setback. It may be hard to do, but at this point your child needs to sense your unwavering love and compassion, not a self-righteous, condemning spirit.

If your child doesn't open up and appears uncomfortable, reaffirm your love and tell her you really want to talk about it when she is ready. Then make sure to follow up within a day or two. If this still fails, go off together to some quiet place and stay there until the lines of communication are defrosted.

On the other hand, if your child expresses a strong commitment to present and future purity, sing the "Hallelujah Chorus," tell her you will pray for her, and offer to show her how she can stay on the path of purity.

GIVE IT SOME THOUGHT

1. Is your child spiritually responsive, wanting to obey God? How do you know? If you aren't sure, how are you going to find out?

2. Is your child in rebellion against God? If so, why? What can you do to help your child toward spiritual restoration?

3. What day-to-day opportunities do you have to explain some of the reasons to wait? How can you begin taking advantage of them?

4. Does your child understand the wisdom of waiting? Does your child view these as a reflection of God's love? If you're not sure, take some time this week to find out. Go some place where you can talk, uninterrupted and undistracted.

5. Does your child plan to wait until marriage to have a sexual relationship? Why not ask? But be sure to prepare yourself for the possible answers.

CHAPTER 8

The Path of Purity

"John, he's pressuring her to have sex. They have already gone too far. If someone doesn't do something soon . . ."

I was concerned, but not surprised. Robert and Heather had dated for close to a year. Whenever our youth group met, they came together. They were inseparable. I had no doubt that she and her boyfriend were committed to Jesus Christ and honestly wanted to wait until marriage to have sex. But despite their commitment, they were years away from marriage and only moments away from intercourse. One of Heather's closest friends was asking me to intervene.

A young person's willingness to accept God's plan for her sexuality by no means guarantees she will follow through on her decision. The decision is only the starting point of what will be a long and certainly difficult path, a path few are willing to walk in the wake of the sexual revolution. Heather and Robert had headed down the dating path with the best of intentions, but they made several wrong turns along the way and found themselves walking into the dead end of sexual sin.

Their first diversion involved underestimating the strength of their sexual desires. When they were together, passion increasingly bonded them like a strong magnet. They never realized how demanding their desires could be.

They made another wrong turn by defining their sexual desires as love. As their passions grew, they believed their love had grown. Love and lust became so identified that Heather and Robert began to believe that their love was the catalyst for their desires. Nothing could have been further from the truth.

When "love" started legitimizing their desires, they took the final turn toward sexual sin. They decided it was no longer necessary to avoid situations where they would be tempted sexually. When they first started dating, they were always in a group, never alone. Later they thought of ingenious ways to isolate themselves so they could pursue their passions unhindered.

I sat down and gently confronted Robert and Heather, reminding them of their commitment to Christ and what that meant for their relationship. I told them how to restore their closeness to the Lord. Fortunately, they responded well to my counsel, especially when I suggested that they talk openly with their parents about their temptations. I even offered to talk to their parents if they didn't!

Like Robert and Heather, Christian teens who decide to wait until marriage for physical intimacy will find more opportunities than they could ever imagine to sacrifice their original commitment to temporary, unbridled pleasure. That's why purity should be viewed as a path with a series of turns that determine the final destination. If a young person makes the right turn at the right time, he will continue on the right road and end up at the right place. But if he makes the wrong turn, he will get on the wrong road to the wrong destination.

As parents, we need to help our children take the right road and stay on it, much as the American Automobile Association (AAA) helps many travelers each year get to their destinations. The AAA supplies maps complete with highlighted directions, estimated mileage between cities and towns, and suggested tourist attractions and motel accommodations. Nothing is left to chance; the trip is carefully planned and clearly plotted. The AAA even stands ready with the tow trucks for any of its members who end up stranded. Similarly, we need to give our children a map, with clear directions and warnings of dangerous roads. We also need always to stand by in case they take a wrong turn or suffer a breakdown. One of the wrong turns we should highlight in red is passion.

DEALING WITH DESIRE

God designed desires into the fabric of our humanity. So in and of themselves, passions are good. But just as our bodies can be used wrongfully, so can our passions.

Desires can bring delight or danger. The danger stems from the world's attempts to give us satisfaction apart from God. But the divinely inspired psalmist tells us, "Delight yourself in the LORD / and He will give you the desires of your heart" (Ps. 37:4). Desires are not wrong, but the way we satisfy them may well be.

Take the desire for significance. If we try to meet this need through the pursuit of success and status, we are looking to the world for fulfillment, not to God. Or how about security? If we look for it in our possessions, we again find ourselves relying on the world, not God. Likewise, when we give our sexual desires free reign with someone other than our spouse, we look away from God and toward worldly pleasure.

Appreciate Passion's Power

My observations sadly verify what one pastor wrote:

> Make no mistake about it—the Christian church is riddled with immorality, among the young and the old, the single and the married, the laity and the leadership. No Christian is immune to sexual temptation. We do ourselves no favor to pretend that the same hormones and human weaknesses common to all people are somehow eradicated when we come to Christ. Enslaved by sexual sin in mind and body, plagued and haunted by its guilt, innumerable children of God are tragically incapacitated in their attempts to live for Christ.
>
> Nothing so hamstrings the believer's spiritual potency as sexual compromise—and never has the church in America been so compromised as now.[1]

Should we be disappointed? Absolutely. Should we be shocked? No. Why not? Because sexual desire can be turned into one of the most destructive forces known to man. Think of the men of Sodom who demanded sexual access to Lot's visitors (Gen. 19). Remember the gang rape of a man's concubine (Judg. 19). Don't forget that David seduced Bathsheba and murdered her husband Uriah to cover up his tracks (2 Sam. 11). Recall the rape of Tamar by her brother Amnon (2 Sam. 13) and remember Solomon, who, although divinely bestowed with the gift of wisdom, took to himself hundreds of wives against the Lord's instruction (1 Kings 11).

The Bible refers to desires that demand gratification apart from

God as lusts. One of these desires is the "lust of the flesh." Lust simply means sinful desire, and flesh refers to our strong inclination to sin. These desires can sever our relationship with God and actually enslave us (Tit. 3:3).

Adolescents and teens have strong sexual desires that are magnified by their youthful energy and insecurity. The apostle Paul understood this, as is indicated in his counsel to young Timothy: "Flee the evil desires of youth. . ." (2 Tim. 2:22). Paul called Timothy's desires evil because Timothy was a bachelor and therefore did not have a legitimate avenue for sexual expression.

Have you forgotten the days of your youth? Think back to your own experience as a teenager. Can't you recall a boy or girl who stirred your sexual passions? How did you handle them? How do you think your child will cope with them?

How strong are the "evil desires" of youth? Having talked openly with many young people, I have concluded that sexual desires dominate the experience of most, especially young men. Aroused by the allurements of our world, their natural inclinations are seldom allowed to subside.

So how can we help them? By getting them started on the road to purity. That path begins when we give our children a healthy appreciation for the intensity of their sex drive. When they were young, we told them that a single match could ignite a fire capable of ravaging an entire household in a matter of minutes. Now they need to know that the flame of passion burning within them can ignite desires that will consume them and those around them. You must explain sexual desires to your children and empathize with their experience. The two obvious questions are when and how.

Only you can tell when your son or daughter has reached the point where puberty has created passion. Given the sexual stimuli that bombard your child daily, it probably will be sooner than you like. A mother who found a condom in the drawer of her twelve-year-old son had waited too long. You can't afford to make the same mistake.

How should you explain these desires to your adolescent or teen? By being honest and biblical.

Begin by showing your child that sexual desire is not wrong, but that satisfying the desires outside of marriage is wrong. Review some of the key passages covered in Chapter 6, especially 1 Corinthians 7:1–4. Point out that God commands a husband and wife to satisfy each other's sexual desires. The desires are not wrong or sinful.

Use biblical examples to show your child the intensity of sexual desires. Turn to the rape of Tamar to communicate this point. Together read 2 Samuel 13:1–19. This tragic account has a wealth of insight for young people whose sexual desires are not unlike those of Amnon. Amnon's desire for Tamar was so great that he "became frustrated to the point of illness on account of his sister Tamar, for she was a virgin, and it seemed impossible for him to do anything to her" (v. 2). Consumed with lust for his half-sister, he spent the night dreaming of sex with her.

Don't discount the rape of Tamar as extreme. Date rape has become an all-too-common occurrence in our day, with television specials and magazine articles chronicling the problem. Sex is expected by many young men; some will not take no for an answer.

Acknowledge Attraction

After your child develops a biblically based understanding of sexual desires, you need to express your sensitivity to the struggles he or she will face in dealing with these desires.

A grandmother who has seventeen granddaughters and fifteen grandsons shared with me a conversation she had with her fourteen-year-old granddaughter. We would do well to follow her example and speak with such honesty and conviction.

> Suzanne, I suppose you've felt excited flutterings when you've been around certain young fellows. Suzanne, don't say "Oh, Grandma." This is an important subject and it would be unnatural if you didn't feel this way.
>
> Even now, though I am so old, I sometimes feel these flutterings when your Grandpa comes in the door. You must have noticed that we like to hold hands and sit close together. This is the way God made people.
>
> God put within us attractions for each other. For proof of this look around you and see that everywhere women enjoy being with men and men want to be with women. The flutterings you feel are good,

natural, and expected. They are the beginning of drawing you to one special person who will be your lifetime mate. You need to acknowledge these good feelings and learn how to control and enjoy them!

What a wonderful expression of sexual attraction! As she said, these are good feelings placed in us by God. Notice how she identified with her granddaughter by unashamedly admitting she still has these same desires.

Explain How Desires Differ

Part of educating our children in their sexuality involves developing their appreciation for the differences between the sexes. While both boys and girls experience strong sexual urges, the way those desires are aroused differs. God recognizes this and encourages each of us to "learn to control his own body in a way that is holy and honorable" (1 Thess. 4:4). How can we teach our children to do this? By teaching them to respond to those desires with appropriate controls.

Boys are easily aroused and are generally more aggressive. In the wake of feminism some have attempted to deny certain sexual distinctives, such as the man being the sexual aggressor. Although there is nothing wrong with a wife initiating sex, God designed the man to be the more aggressive of the sexes.

A young man in his adolescent and teenage years will soon discover that he can get an erection while simply thinking about girls. It takes only sixty seconds for him to be biologically ready to have sex. Before long he will also recognize that he experiences erections spontaneously without any apparent stimulation. These erections occur frequently and can be embarrassing, but they are perfectly natural. Assure your son that if he has a spontaneous erection around children or other boys it does not indicate that he has a strange sexual orientation.

How then do we tell a son how to control his vessel in a holy and honorable way? First of all, point out that his sex drive is the product of male hormones that create internal pressure to release semen. Get a good book that describes the male anatomy, and explain exactly how the system works.

Second, explain that his desires will be intensified if he allows his mind to be filled with sexual information. The more he thinks about sex, the more intense will be the desire for physical release, especially when the visual or audio stimulation causes an erection. He can reduce the frustration of unfulfilled desires by controlling the information that stimulates those desires.

Third, make sure your son knows about nocturnal emissions—wet dreams. God designed his body to ejaculate semen at night during sleep. If it happens, he must understand that it's nothing to be ashamed of. It is God's provision of sexual relief to males. It releases sexual pressure, thereby providing a natural, healthy control of their sexual longings.

Finally, the topic of masturbation will also need to be covered with your son. But since I discuss it at length in Chapter 11, I won't repeat myself here. However, as your child gets older, you will have to help him decide if masturbation is a holy and honorable way to control his sexual desires.

Girls are relationally oriented. Like boys, girls have strong sexual desires of their own. The Scriptures chronicle this. For example, Potiphar's wife attacked Joseph (Gen. 39:7). The apostle Paul told Timothy not to put younger widows on the list for church support because "when their sensual desires overcome their dedication to Christ, they want to marry" (1 Tim. 5:11). (Did you notice that the biblical solution for a widow's intense sexual desires is to get married, not to get a live-in boyfriend?)

Nevertheless, women are not as naturally aggressive as men. As I mentioned before, reported cases of a woman raping a man are few and far between. Let's not ignore the obvious. External genitalia and testosterone cause men to function differently from women. Your daughter should understand the differences between the sexes, not only to comprehend her sexuality, but also to become sensitive to the struggles young men face.

Especially emphasize her vulnerability in relationships. I have lost count of the number of young women I have observed or heard about who in a desperate desire to feel loved have given sex. Typically, they were compelled by years of craving their father's love. A love they longed for, but never received.

At a conference for a group of high school students, I saw a young couple leave the group and take off into the woods. I felt an obligation to follow and make sure that nothing inappropriate happened. I certainly wouldn't expect a Christian camp to allow my son or daughter to go off in the woods to do whatever he or she wanted.

At the counselors' meeting later that day, we discussed the situation and were told this girl had a problem being promiscuous. Her father was an undercover narcotics agent who was seldom at home. This girl didn't receive adequate attention from her dad, and everything she did was an attempt to experience the love she longed to receive from him. At dinner that night, I tried to say a few kind words to this emotionally crippled young girl. I could see confusion in her eyes and sense the heartbreak in her voice.

But even a girl who feels the love of her mom and dad can give in to sexual desires to maintain a relationship. Women, young and old alike, long to be loved, so much so, in fact, that many fall for the age-old line, "If you really loved me, you would." The girl who understands that her emotional needs make her vulnerable has a great chance to walk the path of purity, especially when she distinguishes lust from love.

LUST AND LOVE

Our society equates feelings, especially sexual feelings, with love. In the minds of many teens, physical attraction and love are the same. In our local grocery store, a young man who saw an attractive girl walk by, stopped and said to his friends, "I think I am in love." They all laughed because deep down they knew that love is far more than physical. But in practice, neither young men nor young women can usually get in touch with this intuition when they are physically attracted to a member of the opposite sex. Their hormones take control while their minds go on vacation.

Love Is Not Lust

Ask your child, "What does it mean to fall in love?" Whenever I pose this question to Christian singles, I get some fascinating feedback. Some describe love as a wonderful disease that everyone tries to catch. Others talk about a fuzzy feeling. When I ask for some elaboration, I find their thinking is as fuzzy as their feelings.

Teach your child the difference between lust and love. If your child can't differentiate between the two, he or she may one day marry a body rather than a person. So you must teach them the difference. Where do you start?

Explaining the meaning of the English term *love* isn't a good place because it dilutes the original meaning of the terms for true love in the New Testament. In English, *love* can be used to describe how we feel about our dog as well as our spouse.

In New Testament times, however, there were several terms used to describe the true essence of love. *Eros* was commonly used in the apostolic age, but, interestingly, the inspired writers never used it. Eros love is love for another person because of the physical pleasure they give. It's a sensuous love that desires personal gratification, not mutual edification or fulfillment.

Eros love dominates our society and is one of the big reasons for today's moral decay. Most Christian singles find themselves fighting to get beyond eros. Their struggle is especially dangerous, for when eros flourishes, it causes the physical dimension to dominate relationships and suppresses any opportunity for real intimacy.

List the dangers of eros love for your child:

- Eros will not last because your desires change over time;
- Eros makes it almost impossible to get to know the other person as something more than a body;
- Eros ends when someone more exciting comes along.

Here's a way to define eros for your child:

In the Bible, love based on sexual desire is not even mentioned. God says love is more than just having sex with another person. Love based on sexual attraction says, "I love you because you excite me." But what happens when a person gets disfigured or grows old or when someone more exciting comes along? As soon as that happens, one person tosses the other person aside like yesterday's newspaper. That's why it's important to understand that physical attraction and love are not the same. To desire someone physically does not mean you really love that person.

If your teen learns to distinguish lust from love, he will take a giant step toward spiritual maturity and personal purity. It's a lesson many older Christians have yet to learn.

Love Is a Decision

Two Greek terms in the New Testament are translated love. The first is *philia,* the love of friendship, companionship, and camaraderie. There is give and take in philia love. Philia love includes a sense of obligation and is superior to eros love, but it still is not the ultimate kind of love.

Christians are to be marked by what God calls *agape* love. This special form of love reflects God's unselfish, unconditional, sacrificial love for us. It's love motivated by the will and intellect rather than emotions, feelings, and desires. We decide to act in a loving way toward another person, not for selfish reasons, but for the other person's benefit—not so we might gain anything, but so we might give everything that's best for the other.

As your child grows up, you need to impress upon him the stark contrast between eros and agape. He needs to know the terms and understand the differences.

Worldly Love (Eros)	Christian Love (Agape)
Based on attraction, emotions, desire	Based on will and intellect
Desires self-satisfaction	Desires to serve another
Continuation dependent on self-satisfaction	Continuation dependent on decision to serve
Does not last	Lasts forever

One of the best ways to explain the unconditional character of agape love to your child is to read 1 Corinthians 13:4–7. Whenever you come to the word *love,* substitute the name of your son or daughter. So you would read, "Katie is patient, Katie is kind," and so on. To contrast agape with eros love, emphasize the phrase "is not self seeking." While eros seeks for self, agape does not.

Use this passage to help your child analyze how she feels about another young person. Also draw on it to help you reveal the nature of someone's love for your child. Then when a young man pressures a Christian girl to have sex, she can remind him that "Love is patient, love is kind. . . . it is not rude, it is not self-seeking. . . . does not delight in evil but rejoices with the truth." With this definition, a girl can ask, "Do you really love me, or do you simply want someone to satisfy your sexual desires?"

Since men tend to struggle more with eros, you must be especially candid with your son:

> *Son, love is far more than physical attraction. As a young man you will find that sexual desires can dominate your relationship with a girl. But it's important that you view a girl, not as an object of your desires, but as a person who is loved by God. You must analyze your feelings and actions to see if they reflect a growing commitment to her as a person.*

I would express my concerns differently to my daughter:

> *Sweetheart, when you care about a young man, you may both think you are in love. But your idea of love and his may be very different. Define love as God does. God says love is how we act toward another person, not merely how we feel about that person. If a young man pressures you to have sex before marriage, he is not expressing the kind of love God wants you to enjoy. If he really loves you God's way, he will do what's best for you, and he will be willing to wait until marriage to have sex.*

Biblically, love is a decision. It's an act of the will and the intellect. It does not depend on feelings or emotions, although these naturally follow. A young person who adopts this divine definition will have the foundation not only for purity but also for a wonderful marriage.

But even after opting for love over lust and being mindful of the power of passion, a young person will still confront a roadblock called temptation. The pull of passion will try to seduce her to abandon love for lust.

TEMPTATION

Temptation is an "opportunity" to have legitimate desires met in an illegitimate way. We want security, so the world invites us to pursue power. We desire physical intimacy, so the world offers us promiscuity. Whenever our desires are pulled by ungodly means of gratification, temptation has exercised its creatively deceptive mental muscle. From a casual innuendo on a television program to a blatant proposition by a prostitute, temptation seeks to entrap and devour its prey—you, me, and our kids.

How does temptation take place? Two ways. It occurs naturally in a world subjected to sin. In our world, temptation is not the exception but the rule. We cannot avoid its advances. No matter where we go or what we do, temptation will be close behind.

Demonic forces are another source of invitation to sin. After being baptized, Jesus Christ went into the mountains and battled with Satan, also called the tempter. Satan tempted Jesus Christ by offering to meet His legitimate desires in illegitimate ways (Matt. 4:1-10). He appeals to our sin nature in much the same way.

Temptation has a magnetic power since it appeals to our natural, God-given desires. It constantly invites us to have our desires met in the wrong way and at the wrong time.

Relentless temptations and the strong sexual desires of youth together form a time bomb none can ignore and few escape.

Fight and Lose

After I taught a lesson on the allurements of sin and our need to run from them, a man came up to me with fire in his eyes. He vehemently contested my understanding of the Scriptures and said we should be strong enough to fight temptation rather than merely flee it. When he left we agreed to disagree.

Several months later this man called and asked to meet with me. In an emotional frenzy, he paced the floor outside my office. The moment he walked in he dumped his problem. The next day he had to appear in court on charges of sexual misconduct with a minor. As he explained it, several weeks before, a mother brought her sixteen-year-old daughter to him for counseling. Although attracted to her in the first few sessions, he still scheduled additional meetings. During their fourth meeting, he surrendered to temptation and molested this unsuspecting teen.

This man learned the hard way. He could have escaped sin's seductive advances by deciding to flee rather than staying to fight.

Flee and Win

I have yet to find a single verse in the Bible that says we should hang around and fight temptation. But I see substantial scriptural evidence for fleeing temptation.

When Paul counseled Timothy, he didn't tell him to stand and fight it off. He said, "Flee the evil desires of youth, and pursue righteousness, faith, love and peace, along with those who call on the Lord out of a pure heart" (2 Tim. 2:22). Evil desires are synonymous with temptation. First Corinthians 10:12–13 adds: "So, if you think you are standing firm, be careful that you don't fall! No temptation has seized you except what is common to man. And God is faithful; he will not let you be tempted beyond what you can bear. But when you are tempted, he will also provide a way out so that you can stand up under it."

When temptation comes pressing down, God provides an escape route, a way to flee so that we don't get imprisoned and crushed. The way out of the temptation is usually offered well in advance of a compromising situation. The first escape hatch is fleeing the mental seduction so prevalent in the media. From commercials to prime time programs, sexual allurements act as visual hooks swallowed by desensitized viewers.

So make sure you teach your child to recognize and run in the face of temptation. Give your child examples of sexual allurements and suggest ways to flee them. A well defined plan will offer your child a great degree of protection.

Don't get me wrong. As a realist I know that young people will be tempted no matter how hard they may try to flee. The world has a way of assaulting their faith and commitment until they give in, emotionally and spiritually exhausted. Neither they nor we have the strength to win the battle with sexual sin on our own. And yet it's precisely at the point of our helplessness that success can be ours. For if we draw on the special power available to us, we can walk the path of purity. What is that power? Let's see.

GIVE IT SOME THOUGHT

1. Is your child experiencing sexual desires? How strong are they?

2. Does your child understand the intensity of the sex drive?

3. Can your child differentiate between love and lust? If not, how do you plan to explain the differences?

4. How does your child define love?

5. Does your child embrace, fight, or flee temptation?

6. Specify some ways your child can run from temptation and think of how you can communicate them to him or her.

CHAPTER 9

The Power for Purity

When I became a Christian, my parents were amazed that their fast-moving son had settled down with a Bible and a commitment to Jesus Christ. My dad was especially puzzled by my new purpose in life. They had taken me to church for years, but nothing like this had ever happened. Now I challenged them to enter into a relationship with Jesus Christ.

One day while casually walking through our family room, I asked my dad, "Are you going to heaven?" He gave me the usual answer: "I think so. . . ." Dissatisfied with that, I went on to explain how he could know for sure.

Shortly after that conversation, my dad challenged my Christianity. On a hot and muggy afternoon with my knuckles bleeding and bruised from feeble attempts to tune my car, I discovered that the clerk at the auto store had given me the wrong spark plugs. I was fit to be tied. My dad came by at just the wrong time and offered to help. His words made matters worse, since I knew he knew nothing about cars. I mumbled, "No, I don't want your help. *I* can take care of it."

But he persisted: "No, son, let me give you a hand."

That's all it took for my emotional engine to overheat. Flippantly I said, "Leave me alone. I'll take care of it."

Immediately he retorted with, "Is this the way Christians act? Is this what your faith is all about?"

When he said that, my razor-sharp tongue wanted to say, "Yes, and if you don't like it—tough!" But as the words started to roll to the tip of my tongue, an incredible power grabbed my heart as well as my lips. It was as if someone had put a vise grip around my anger. Instead of firing back, I asked for forgiveness. I apologized for my attitude and what I had said.

That day my father saw something in me that he had never seen before. It confirmed in his mind that something had taken place within me that was nothing short of supernatural. Several months later he came to trust in Jesus Christ as his Savior and Lord.

I learned two critical lessons that day. I discovered that even as a Christian, my temper still existed and could surface and gain control over me. I still had the capacity to explode with anger even when someone's eternal destiny was at stake. And yet, while I learned that my B.C. (Before Christ) behavior still lived, I also found a new power present—a power that allowed me to respond differently than I would have before becoming a Christian.

My struggle that day parallels what our children deal with when they decide to walk the path of purity. Intense sexual desires strive to gain control. Lust fights to replace true love. A voice within encourages surrender to the tug of temptation.

A war is being waged within each of our children. In this war, sexual desires battle with the desire to please God. Understanding these desires, knowing that love differs from lust, and predeciding to flee temptation all provide us with a strategy and a plan of action. But in themselves, they do not give us the power to win the war.

THE WAR WITHIN YOUR CHILD

The Christian life is a moment-by-moment battle played out in the arena of relationships. The stakes are high. Defeat comes at a great price. If we lose, we lose life as it was meant to be.

Our opponent stands as a Goliath ready to engage in hand-to-hand combat. What makes fighting this giant especially difficult is that he lives within us. Wherever we go, he is there waiting for an opportunity to assert his overwhelming power. He has several names: the old man, our old self, our sin nature, and the flesh. He is ugly because there's nothing good about him. His portrait is found in several of Paul's letters. Paul knew him well. And as a military man, Paul knew that our success in battle largely depends on our knowledge of this enemy. "You were taught, with regard to your former way of life, to put off your old self, which is being corrupted by its deceitful desires; to be made new in the attitude of your minds; and to put on the new self, created to be like God in true righteousness and holiness" (Eph. 4:22–24).

Note the contrast Paul makes in this passage. The old or former way of life stands in opposition to the new life or to a new self. Although we become a new creature in Christ when we believe in Him for our salvation, our old tendency to sin still exists in us. In order to live out our new life, we must discard our old ways and replace them with the new ways laid out in Scripture. But we quickly discover that this is more easily said than done. Our "deceitful desires" keep pulling us toward our former way of life. Why? Because our passion for sin is woven into the fabric of our fallen humanity. Until our death and resurrection usher in the fullness of our redemption, we will continue to lose battles with our bent to do evil. Even the apostle Paul lost some battles with the "Old Paul": "I do not understand what I do. For what I want to do I do not do, but what I hate I do. . . . I know that nothing good lives in me, that is, in my sinful nature. For I have the desire to do what is good, but I cannot carry it out. For what I do is not the good I want to do; no, the evil I do not want to do—this I keep on doing" (Rom. 7:15,18–19).

Paul's words have been my words on many occasions. I know what I should do, and I want to do it. But I often end up doing what is wrong. I walk away frustrated and defeated.

Have you been there? I know you have. But have you ever thought that your bouts with sin are comparable to your child's battles with sexual sin?

Your Child's Struggle with Sin

Many Christian young people feel like Paul. In their struggle with sexual sin, they know what is right, and they want to do what is right. But they end up doing what is wrong. I frequently hear kids say, "I had the desire to wait until marriage, but I could not carry it out." Like us, our children have competing desires waging war within them. And like us, their desire to do what is wrong is often more powerful than their desire to do what is right. In themselves, they do not have the internal resources to follow through on their decision to live for God.

Do you realize that none of us has the spiritual strength to overcome our sin nature? If Paul couldn't defeat it, neither can we. As far as he was concerned, the "old Paul" clung to his back like a Suma wrestler. No matter how hard Paul tried, his old ways would bear down upon him, trying to take him down, pin him, and crush him. In frustration Paul cried out for help, "What a wretched man I am! Who will rescue me from this body of death?" (Rom. 7:24).

Does your child understand the propensity to sin that exists within us all? Most don't. Therefore, they find themselves confused and overwhelmed when illicit desires surface with increasing strength and regularity. Many Christian young people have never been told about the battle that goes on within every believer. They don't realize they have a tendency to sin which wars against their new spiritual nature. So they walk around defenseless, easy prey for the assaults of sin. No wonder in their adolescent and teen years they usually surrender to the opponent of their purity, never realizing he is an enemy from within who brings temporary pleasure laced with heartache and destruction.

So how can you help your child to understand this internal struggle? Here's a simple explanation I would use to help my child understand what the Bible calls the flesh, the old self, or the sin nature. After reading some of the important passages together, I would summarize their meaning this way:

Have you found that even when you want to do what's right you still sometimes do what's wrong? It's as if there are two voices that whisper in your ear, each directing you a different way. For example, I know I shouldn't be as impatient with you as I am at times. I get angry and I know it's wrong; I blow up at you and later regret it. That's my sin nature. It's a part of me that wants to disobey God. It's a strong tendency to sin, even when I don't want to sin.

You have this same nature in you. You will decide to wait until marriage to have sex, but your sin nature will plant the thought that you should do what you want and forget what God says. It will be a voice inside of you that tells you to disobey God. As a Christian you must decide if you are going to do what your old sin nature says or do what your new nature as a believer says.

If our children are to identify and defeat the enemy within, they must be able to recognize the signs of his control. Paul lays them bare: "The acts of the sinful nature are obvious: sexual immorality, impurity and debauchery; idolatry and witchcraft; hatred, discord, jealousy, fits of rage, selfish ambition, dissensions, factions and envy; drunkenness, orgies, and the like" (Gal. 5:19,20).

Have you ever taken your child's spiritual temperature? Just run down Paul's list and see how many of the characteristics mentioned describe your child. Note also that these behaviors have their roots in the spiritual, not the psychological. They exist ultimately because the sin nature exists, not simply because of some past trauma or experience. Even if your child grew up in a "perfect" home, the sins of the flesh would still arise. Psychology can help you understand why your child is prone to commit certain sins, but it will not take you to the source of her actions. So for a long-lasting solution to your kid's misbehavior, you need to look beyond her psyche and past and see the condition of her spirit. You must teach her how to defeat the sin nature that dwells within so she can walk the path of purity. If she decides to put off her former self for the person she is in Christ, she will not allow the sin nature to carry her into "sexual immorality, impurity, and . . . orgies."

There is, however, one serious problem. Even if she wants to overcome her sin nature, she doesn't have the personal strength to do so. Recall what the apostle Paul said: "I have the desire to do what is good, but I cannot carry it out" (Rom. 7:18). Does that mean your Christian child is doomed to defeat, especially in a day when monogamy is thought to be a new game by Milton Bradley? Yes and no. Yes, they will lose somewhere down the line if they try to battle their sin nature in their own power. No, they will not lose the war if they appropriate a power capable of overcoming the youthful passions being fed by our sex-saturated society.

What is this power? Jesus Christ spoke of it when He said, "Apart from me you can do nothing" (John 15:5). Paul knew that the believers in Ephesus needed outside assistance, so he prayed, "Out of his glorious riches he (God) may strengthen you with power. . ." (Eph. 3:16). Our children can—and must—have that supernatural power if they are going to walk the path of purity. That source of sin-breaking strength is the Holy Spirit.

But it's obvious that few Christian young people tap into His power to overcome their sin nature. When the percentage of Christian youth involved sexually outside of marriage does not differ significantly from that of their peers, we can be sure they are living according to their sin nature, not according to the Spirit's power. But why? Why are our young people suffering from spiritual anemia?

For one thing, their spiritual weakness usually mirrors spiritually weak parents. Many of us feel comfortable living according to our sin nature. We no longer fight off its promptings. Our children see that and so inherit our spiritual condition almost by default. For another, few of us understand that the Christian life is impossible apart from the power of God. We are attempting to live biblically in our own strength which the Bible tells us we can't. And finally, we do not understand the Person of power who lives within every believer. If we did and if we were communicating that knowledge to our kids so they could understand and apply it, far fewer of them would be falling victim to their old nature.

THE HOLY SPIRIT AND YOUR CHILD

What difference does the Holy Spirit make in your life? We all know He should make a difference and we sense He has made a difference, but we also know that the difference we experience does not equal the One who lives within us. When the God of the universe takes up residency in our lives, something has to happen. And yet, many of us suffer from a severe case of spiritual atrophy. After an initial spasm of change following conversion, we find ourselves with a deep longing for the reality of the Spirit's work in our lives. The same holds true for our kids.

A friend of mine defines the Christian life as "the life of Christ reproduced in the believer by the power of the Holy Spirit in obedient response to the Word of God." For most of this book I have concentrated on the whats, whys, and hows of teaching and challenging your child to obey the Word of God. Now I want to focus on the power that will make your child's obedience to God possible.

Anyone who places faith in Jesus Christ receives the Holy Spirit, also called the Spirit of Christ. "And if anyone does not have the Spirit of Christ, he does not belong to Christ" (Rom. 8:9). Children who become Christians have the Holy Spirit within them to comfort, direct, guide, and empower them. But few Christian children understand the presence of the Holy Spirit and the power available to them through Him.

It's been said that what's fuzzy for the teacher will be a blur to the pupil. That may well describe why most Christian children don't have a basic appreciation for the person and work of the Holy Spirit. Many of us are confused and uncertain about the Spirit's ministry. Let me ask you, How does the Holy Spirit help you to have victory over your old nature? If you have a ready answer, you are a breed apart. May your family be blessed as a result! If you didn't have an answer, welcome to the club, but don't stay a member. Use the rest of this chapter as your teacher's manual for the ABCs of the Spirit. Don't allow your ignorance to jeopardize the spiritual life of your child.

The Holy Spirit Within Your Child

Several passages teach that the Holy Spirit is God's gift to every believer. Shortly before His death, Jesus said, "Whoever believes in me, as the Scripture has said, streams of living water will flow from within him. By this he meant the Spirit, whom those who believed in Him were later to receive" (John 7:38,39). In his letter to the Romans Paul wrote, "God has poured out His love into our hearts by the Holy Spirit, whom He has given us" (Rom. 5:5). Even in the Corinthian Church where sexual sin, including incest (chapter 5), flourished, believers were told that the Holy Spirit lives "in" them. "Do you not know that your body is a temple of the Holy Spirit, who is in you, whom you have received from God?" (1 Cor. 6:19). When Paul asked that question of the believers, it was because they were using their bodies to engage in sexual sin. He wanted them to remember that the Holy Spirit was with them even during the illicit act.

How can you explain the "indwelling" of the Holy Spirit to your child? Use the common phenomenon of wind to describe the movement of the Spirit. We cannot see air. Yet we must breath it in or die. We cannot see the wind, but we know it makes things move in different directions. In fact, it has incredible power—the power to move ships, to level buildings, to bring life-giving rain. Like air and the wind, the Holy Spirit cannot be seen. He doesn't have a body because He is a spirit. We know He exists, because the Scriptures tell us He does and because we have witnessed His incredible power to transform lives, including our own.

You can use numerous other examples to demonstrate the reality of the Holy Spirit to your child. You can show your child how Peter before Pentecost denied the Lord three times, then after receiving the Spirit, boldly preached to over three thousand people. You can chronicle Paul's transformation following his conversion. Beyond the biblical record, you can read the biographies of great Christians who walked in the power of the Holy Spirit. You can also point out people today who exhibit the supernatural power of the Spirit in their daily lives. The illustrations at your disposal are plentiful. All you need to do is use them to help your child understand who the Spirit is and what He can do in a person's life *if submission takes place*.

Your Child Under the Holy Spirit's Control

You see, ideally Christian children "are controlled not by the sinful nature but by the Spirit . . ." (Rom. 8:9). Usually, however, this doesn't occur. Why? The answer revolves around the issue of control. Our children's sin nature fights their new nature for control. But the new nature in itself lacks the power to defeat the sin nature. At the same time, the Holy Spirit waits to be given the opportunity to control and empower the new nature to do what is right. And that opportunity can only be given by our children. They must be willing to surrender to the Spirit, not to sin.

Our children can live under the control of their sin nature which thrives on sexual sin, or they can live under the control of the Holy Spirit who provides the power for purity. Our children have a choice. They can decide to live according to their flesh. Or they can decide to live according to the Spirit. Our responsibility is to explain what their choices are, then challenge them to do what's right. We cannot force them to make the right choice. God will not force them either.

But how do we know when the Spirit has control? What does His control look like? Since we can't see Him, we must look for His effects. The Bible calls them fruit. While the fruit of our sin nature includes sexual immorality, impurity, and orgies, the fruit of the Spirit includes "love, joy, peace, patience, kindness, goodness, faithfulness, gentleness and self control" (Gal. 5:19–23). The fruit of the Spirit counters the old sin nature. Rather than sexual immorality, He produces self-control. In place of lust, the Spirit brings about true love. For the teenager who struggles with waiting until marriage, the Spirit gives patience. For the young man who might be prone to force himself on his date, the Spirit works to produce kindness and goodness.

How does the Holy Spirit's control take place? Do we have to do something? Or does it just happen?

The Spirit's control takes place in the context of a relationship. Since the Holy Spirit is a person, He has a mind (Rom. 8:27) and the ability to be disappointed with us or grieved by our actions (Eph. 4:30). He can be lied to (Acts 5:1–11) and His work resisted (Acts 7:51). He can tell us what to do, and we can obey or disobey Him (Acts 10:19). Although the purpose of the Holy Spirit's ministry is to help us develop our relationship with the Savior, we do sustain a distinct relationship with the Spirit as well.

Concerning our children, two primary factors determine the effectiveness of our children's relationship with the Holy Spirit. The first is their knowledge of God's Word, which was written under the inspiration of the Spirit (2 Peter 1:20,21) and is called the "sword of the Spirit" (Eph. 6:17). The second is their sensitivity to the Spirit's promptings.

Relationships require mutual understanding built through communication. Shortly after Teri and I met, she went back to college. While there she sent me a note I practically memorized. Why? Because we were entering into a relationship, and I wanted to know how she felt about me—about us. When she came back home and we went out together, she naturally assumed I had read her letter and knew how she felt. Likewise, God gave us the Bible as both a message of His love for us and a manual for us to live by. The Holy Spirit produced and preserved it for us. The Scriptures bear His supernatural character and divine fingerprints. He uses the Bible to teach, rebuke, correct, and train us in righteousness (2 Tim. 3:16). But if we don't know His Word, we undercut the transformation process He longs to accomplish in us (Rom. 12:2). For you see, the tool for change He uses most in our lives is the Bible.

Even in Old Testament times, the Scriptures were seen as the divine means to produce personal purity:

> How can a young man keep his way pure?
> By living according to your word.
> I seek you with all my heart;
> do not let me stray from your commands.
> (Psalm 119:9–10)

Beyond the Word of God, the Holy Spirit prompts us to live that which we have learned. The moment we begin to operate according to our sin nature, He whispers, "Don't." When we begin to fall into sin, He says, "Stop." When we are ready to blow up at our kids, He says "Be patient." When we are tempted to sin sexually, He says, "Flee." You know you've heard His voice, but does your child hear Him as well?

Although Eli the high priest was an undisciplined and delinquent father, he showed one spark of parental genius. After Hannah brought her son, Samuel, to the temple, he came under the less-than-capable care of Eli. One night while sleeping in the temple, Samuel heard a voice and thought it was Eli. But the voice was not Eli's. This happened three times before Eli finally realized Samuel was hearing the voice of God. He told Samuel to go back and lie down and when he heard the voice again to say, "Speak, LORD, for your servant is listening" (1 Sam. 3:9).

While we should not necessarily expect to hear an audible voice as Samuel did, we can expect the Spirit to impress upon us His desires for our lives. You probably won't hear a thing with your physical ears, but you will hear in your spirit, your inner ear, the Holy Spirit's call for you to obey the Scriptures He has given.

Perhaps you have never experienced the work of the Spirit as I have described it. If not, I would encourage you to make certain that you have put your personal faith in Jesus Christ "because those who are led by the Spirit of God are sons of God" (Rom. 8:14). Or it may be that you are a Christian and have been led by the Spirit without realizing it. Now is the time to develop your relationship with Him as you encourage your children to do the same.

Christians, regardless of age, should strive to understand the ministry of the Holy Spirit in their lives. The incredible struggles our young people face demand the supernatural intervention of the Holy Spirit. As they grow in their knowledge of Him and become sensitive to His presence and promptings, they will have a ready companion who will help them on the long and difficult path to purity. He will always be there—even when we as parents cannot be. And He can always give them a power we don't naturally possess.

APPROPRIATING THE SPIRIT'S POWER

How does a relationship with the Holy Spirit provide the power for a young person to live a holy life? Or, how can a teenager be filled with the Spirit and thereby come under His control?

The clearest statement about the empowering or filling of the Spirit is Ephesians 5:15–18: "Be very careful, then, how you live—not as unwise but as wise, making the most of every opportunity, because the days are evil. Therefore, do not be foolish, but understand what the Lord's will is. Do not get drunk on wine, which leads to debauchery. Instead, be filled with the Spirit."

The careful, wise walk of a believer becomes all the more difficult and essential in the evil days in which we live. After making this important point, Paul says that we should not come under the influence of wine but should be filled with the Spirit. The present tense used for the word *filled* indicates Spirit control is not a once-and-for-all event. It is something that must be repeated.

The contrasts and similarities between the effects of alcohol and the control of the Spirit provide important critical insights. Both alcohol and the Spirit determine a person's behavior. Alcohol controls the drinker's thinking and dictates his actions, but not apart from his choice. When someone gets drunk, he consciously decides to place himself under the influence of alcohol.

The Spirit's filling also controls our behavior. But unlike alcohol, His control is for our good and results in a Christlike character and healthy relationships. His control overrides the negative influence of our sin nature. The bottom line? Either our old nature or the Holy Spirit will direct our lives.

But how do we come under the control of the Spirit? By making a conscious choice. We decide to yield or submit to the Spirit, just as we can decide to yield to the influence of alcohol. It's our decision—no one else's.

Likewise, children can submit themselves to their sin nature or to the Word of God and the power of the Holy Spirit. The choice they make will determine their sexual behavior.

Developing Your Child's Sensitivity to the Holy Spirit

After my children came to know the Lord, I looked for opportunities to teach them about the ministry of the Holy Spirit. When my son was just six years old, we had a choice teachable moment on a visit to my wife's parents.

The people next door were building their house and had surveyors' sticks along the edge of the property. While my son and I were playing in the fresh mountain air, he noticed the sticks with the intriguing flags. I explained to him why they were there and told him not to touch them. After going in the house for a moment, I returned to find my son waving one of the surveyor's flags. I said, "Why did you pick that up when I told you not to?"

He caught me off guard when he said, "Something in my head told me to do it."

His big blue eyes almost melted me, but I pressed on. "Didn't something in your head tell you *not* to do it?" He nodded yes. "So you listened to the wrong voice, right?" A downcast glance gave me his answer.

So we sat down and had a good talk on what had happened and why. I reminded him that the Bible tells us what we should and should not do. I told him there was a part of him that does not want to obey God. Then I explained that the voice in his head that told him not to touch the flag was God, the Holy Spirit, who lives in him because he is a Christian. "Son," I concluded, "God would have helped you do what was right if you had only asked Him to."

By helping our children become sensitive to the Spirit, we launch them into the Spirit-filled life. That was Paul's intention with the Corinthian believers: "Flee from sexual immorality. All other sins a man commits are outside his body, but he who sins sexually sins against his own body. Do you not know that your body is a temple of the Holy Spirit, who is in you, whom you have received from God? You are not your own; you were bought at a price. Therefore honor God with your body" (1 Cor. 6:18–20).

Sexual sin involves our body, which is the sacred residence of the

Holy Spirit. So when we sin sexually, we have the Holy Spirit right
there with us, offering to help us do what is right.

Here's how I try to make this point with an adolescent or teenage
boy:

> *God, the Holy Spirit, lives within you. He wants to help you do*
> *what God has commanded you to do. When you find yourself looking*
> *at a girl the wrong way, He will let you know you should stop. You*
> *can ignore Him or obey Him. When you are out with a girl and you*
> *start to get tempted, He will tell you to stop and flee.*
>
> *Don't let your heart grow cold to the Spirit. When you find your-*
> *self having to choose between right and wrong, just ask Him for His*
> *help, and His power will flow to and through you. When you call on*
> *Him, He will give you patience and self-control so you can live for*
> *the Lord.*

Teaching Your Child to Walk in the Power of the Holy Spirit

How do we actually receive the Spirit's power? It's no secret. We
receive His power by asking for it and yielding to it at the time we
need it.

As I have fought and continue to fight my own sin nature, I have
found that the filling of the Spirit occurs when I sense my need for
help and call upon the Lord to provide that help. When my short
fuse begins to burn, if I cry out, "Lord help me," He always does.
If I call to Him when my eyes begin to feed my lusts, my sin nature
loses and my new nature wins. I don't always call on Him when I
should, but when I do, He somehow pours on the power to bring me
victory.

Incidentally, I have studied the times I have failed to turn to Him
and discovered they occur when I have not been worshiping, studying the Bible, or praying consistently. In other words, when I have
not taken the time to cultivate my spiritual life, I become less sensitive to the Spirit's presence and don't appropriate His power.

From my personal experience, I would explain the operation of
the Spirit's power to my child this way:

> *When the wrong desires begin to surface in your mind, they must*
> *be put aside. But as you know, that's not easy to do. In fact, it's very*

difficult. You will find yourself at a point of crisis in which you know you can decide to do what is right or decide to do what is wrong. If at that moment you ask the Lord to direct and influence you, He will give you His power to do what you should.

If your spiritual life is the pits because you have not been praying or studying the Scriptures as you should, then you will stand a good chance of not even bothering to ask for the Spirit's help. That's why you should strive to grow spiritually every day so that you will stay in tune with your source of strength.

I have only scratched the surface of the Spirit's ministry, but I hope I have imparted a vision to you for teaching your child about God's power for purity.

I have never heard this subject addressed relative to raising children. Recognizing its obvious importance, I can only conclude that this omission has created a stronghold of the enemy. It's time we as parents teach our children how they can live the Christian life in the power of the Holy Spirit as they respond obediently to God's Word. And we need to start this educational process in the early years of their lives.

GIVE IT SOME THOUGHT

1. Is your child a Christian? Have you seen evidence of the Spirit's work in his or her life?

2. Does your child understand the person and work of the Holy Spirit? How do you know?

3. Does your child understand the relationship of the Bible to the Holy Spirit?

4. Is your child sensitive to the Holy Spirit's leading?

5. How can you help your child gain a greater sensitivity to the Holy Spirit?

CHAPTER 10

Preparation—The Early Years

When should I start to talk to my child about sex? That's the pressing question for many parents, especially those with young children. In a way, however, "When?" is a moot question, because we already have started to teach our children about sex. Even if we have engaged in a conspiracy of silence, our actions and attitudes have shouted louder than any words.

Sex education starts at birth (maybe even before!). A child's life begins as the product of a sexual union. Conception codes the child for life as being male or female. Once the child is born, nurturing takes place at a mother's breast in an expression of shared sexuality.

Then, in the early years, a child learns from observation. A little boy sees Dad has a penis like his and wonders what happened to Mom's. A little girl discovers Dad has a penis and wonders why she doesn't.

Infants, toddlers, and preschoolers develop their basic perceptions of sexuality from observations made in the home. These early attitudes become a pair of glasses through which they will interpret their sexual identity. Their attitudes and perceptions are indelibly marked by our model of sexuality. We plant in their minds a basic understanding of their sexuality, hopefully sending down roots of appreciation for their maleness or femaleness.

Similarly, in their younger years we can begin training their inner ears to discern which voice to heed—the one prompting them to do what's right or the one urging them to do what's wrong. They may one day decide to turn away from God and us, but they cannot walk away from the whispers within. As their minds replay the tapes of the past, they will hear our words, telling them about His Word and the Spirit's words reinforcing ours. As Christian educators Kenneth and Elizabeth Gangel note: "There is no comparable period of life during which a person learns more and progresses more rapidly than the three years immediately prior to entering school. It is *the* time when parents have their greatest opportunity to determine the values and life-style of their children."[1]

WHEN SHOULD SEX EDUCATION BEGIN?

Ideally, we should teach our children about sex at a pace appropriate for their intellectual, emotional, and spiritual development. The amount of information we communicate should be determined by their ability to comprehend. Unfortunately, our sex-crazed society does not allow us the luxury of waiting. We feel rushed to say something before someone else does. We fear our children's innocence will be betrayed if we wait too long and they hear the "facts" from a misinformed friend. So we must begin early, even at birth.

When Your Child Is Born

Whoever said it first said it well: "Sex is not what we do; sex is what we are." Even before a child comes into the world, gender has been the object of concern and prayer. The parents of three boys are praying, maybe begging, God for a girl. Parents who have girls don't realize how good they have had it, so they pray for a boy.

When a child is born, the doctor proclaims with a sense of victory, "It's a _____!" Sex education has begun. In a matter of minutes grandparents, aunts, uncles, and friends across the country have heard the good news, "It's a boy!" "It's a girl!"

The newborn experiences the embrace of Mom and Dad just moments after birth, being kissed and hugged while feeding at Mom's breast. A soft, blue blanket is a mantle of maleness, while a delicate pink blanket is proof positive of a pretty baby girl.

Education by association is another hallmark of childhood sexual development. The breast-fed baby associates warmth and security with being full and satisfied. Toilet training allows a toddler to experience parental acceptance while discovering self-control. For toddlers and preschoolers alike, lessons in hygiene communicate the sanctity of their bodies. These positive associations (and many others) configure a child's initial perception of sex. So this mental and emotional network of experiences must be positive and directed Godward. At the youngest possible age, kids should be convinced they are gifts from God and their bodies are special, having been made by the Creator Himself.

When Pressured to Protect

Have you been shocked to find your child assaulted with information from their peers or the media? One mother shared with me her frustration: "I teach my child to be chaste and modest and to use proper words for the body parts. It seems it is all futile when I hear the words she comes home with after being at school or a friend's house. These are the 'nice' children she plays with. I know their parents. Where do they hear this filthy and degrading language?"

Another letter along this same line is indicative of the kind of pressures little children face in some public schools: "My daughter will soon be seven years old and has attended public school for two years (kindergarten and first grade). She knows every cuss word and has been chased by boys who want to 'kiss her private place.' What kind of people are we? I am alarmed and don't know exactly what to teach her in view of my own ignorance."

So when do you tell your child the facts of life? I have several principles to help you answer this question. First, *be the one to tell your child about sex before someone else does*. You are the in-house sex expert. Anything your child wants to know about sex should come from your mouth, not someone else's. But at the same time, you do not want to give them explicit sexual information sooner than necessary.

Second, *ideally, instruction should be determined on the basis of your child's need to know*. But our society is forcing us to tell our kids sooner. Therefore, *you need to gauge your conversations by the degree to which you can protect your child from outside "enlightenment."* For example, a child who watches little or no television and is home schooled can usually be taught at a slower pace. By contrast, a child who watches a lot of television and attends a public school in a large city needs an advanced course in human sexuality in the earliest grades.

Unfortunately, regardless of your efforts to protect your child, you will not be able to control completely what they hear from their peers. When my son was just six years old, a boy from another Christian home called him a name, using a slang term. When this boy's mother found out, she was mortified that her "cherub" was using gutter terms. During her follow-up investigation, she learned her ten-year-old son had picked the word up in school and passed it on to his little brother. So the term traveled from the local school to her ten-year-old, who told his six-year-old brother, who then told my son. That's the reality of our day. We may not like it, but we must live with it.

However, you don't need to permit happenings like this to panic you into flooding your kid's mind with information he or she can't process. You can delay telling your child more than he or she really needs to know about sex. How? *By warning your child that some people use the wrong words to describe the private parts of the body, and that these people do not understand the wonderful way God uses a mom's and a dad's body to create a baby.* Here's one way you can warn your child:

There are people who do not understand the special way God has made us. They use dirty and unkind words to describe a penis or a vagina. Now, I know all the words, and when you get older we can talk about them. Until then, the Lord wants you to keep these words out of your mind, so don't worry about them right now. These people also don't understand the beautiful way God uses a mom's body and a dad's to create a baby.

So when you hear someone talk this way, ignore them, walk away from them, and be sure to tell me about them right away. Remember, I never want you to be afraid to tell Mom or me anything you hear.

Alerting your child to the unsavory thoughts and words of others makes you a prophet in his or her sight. Predicting what others will say confirms your wisdom. It also allows you to postpone graphic discussions until they are absolutely necessary.

A mother shared with me how this approach worked for her family:

While at the community swimming pool, two little girls accused my seven-year-old son of saying the "F" word. Although they were just seven or eight years old, these little girls felt very comfortable using

the slang term for intercourse in front of me and were shocked when
I told them that my son did not know the word. Later my son came up
to me all upset and said, "Mom, those girls said I said the 'F' word."
I probed, asking, "What's the 'F' word?" He responded. "They said
I said, '*Fart* you.'" After I explained that these girls used the wrong
word for intercourse, he immediately said, "That's one of those
words Dad said he would tell me about later on, isn't it?"

This warning system maintains a parent's credibility and also
preserves a child's innocence for as long as possible—innocence
our world seems destined to destroy.

When Development Demands It

While we seek to guard our children from the assault of explicit
information, we do not countenance ignorance. As they mature, we
must explain the changes that take place in their bodies as well as in
their minds.

I have been amazed to hear from a number of women who as
young girls were never told about menstruation, then had their first
menstrual period while at school. As one woman remembered, "I
was in the fifth grade and went to the restroom in the middle of
math class. I looked down and literally thought I was going to die."

While girls need to be informed on menstruation, wet dreams or
nocturnal emissions must be explained to boys. A boy can wake up
in the morning finding himself in a pool of semen. A friend told me
that when he was a boy, he woke himself up early every morning in
order to have enough time to clean his sheets before going to
school. He thought he was wetting the bed when he was only having
an occasional nocturnal emission.

As you observe anatomical developments during puberty, make
certain your child understands the biological changes that are taking
place. Don't cause your child unnecessary fear or embarrassment.
When their development demands it—speak.

When Opportunity Invites It

When children want information, they usually ask for it. What
child has not asked why Dad has a penis and Mom doesn't? What
child hasn't asked where babies come from? The curiosity behind a

question ought to be satisfied with a simple, honest, accurate, and biblical answer.

You should not read too much into a child's question. Neither should you overload your child with an exhaustive or high-powered answer. Usually a concise explanation satisfies a child's interest. A preschooler who asks where babies come from does not need to know the specifics of intercourse. Describing the uterus or womb as the place where the baby grows until being born will typically satisfy the child's curiosity.

In addition to answering questions, there are teachable moments when sex education will be most effective. On one of our many trips to the local zoo, my then three-year-old son ran ahead of Teri and me to see the large tortoises who lived on a small island. I lingered behind, preoccupied with my Sunday sermon. Then he yelled to me, "Dad, what are they doing?" I awoke out of my comatose state to see two three-hundred-pound tortoises copulating. I had a choice opportunity to talk about reproduction, but instead, coming out of my daze, I said, "I think they are playing." What a lousy answer! I missed a teachable moment.

Life in the home presents its own set of teachable moments. Breeding the family dog gives a close-up look at the beauty of birth. One day my children came bouncing through our back door with the news that Chelsea, our friend's dog, had puppies. They told me how the puppies came out and started to nurse. They were absolutely fascinated. With their interest piqued, I drew parallels to when a person is born. Although at that moment they were more interested in the puppies, we referred back to Chelsea and her babies years later to explain the plan for reproduction and the beauty of birth.

A more advanced course in human sexuality can flow from the anticipation and preparation for a new baby. I can still remember the lessons we taught our oldest when Teri was pregnant with our second child. We reinforced in his young mind that both he and this baby were gifts from God and that God had used our bodies to give them life.

HOW DO YOU TEACH YOUR CHILD?

A friend of mine who has five children told me the story of his "big talk" with his oldest son who was going off to camp. He and his wife agreed that their son needed to be told about sex since something inappropriate could happen during the boy's time away. My highly successful, gregarious friend described his anxiety in talking with his boy. Later, Mom who has been trained as a nurse asked the boy a few simple questions which he could not answer. She then asked her husband what the two of them talked about. Under her interrogation, he admitted that all he did was warn his son about deviants who might try to touch him. His wife couldn't believe that's all he accomplished with the "big talk."

The big talk has never worked well. It needs to be replaced by short, simple exchanges that occur naturally. But never forget— your attitudes and actions speak more than your words.

Affection

Children who experience warmth and tenderness in their relationship with their parents are being bathed in acceptance. Affection is to children's self-esteem and emotions what food is to their body. Every embrace tells them they are loved as persons, as boys or girls. Their self-perceptions are reinforced. They become more and more comfortable with their sexuality. This kind of affection is not overbearing or smothering; rather, it's a natural expression of agape love.

Jesus Christ modeled a healthy affection for children. While his disciples tried to turn children away, Jesus embraced them and used them to illustrate the essence of faith.

When our children were very little, we started what we call a "family hug." Teri and I would each lift a child, then embrace each other. It was a great idea until the children got so big they were causing us back problems!

However you express affection in your home, be sure to do it often. And don't forget to express it to your spouse in front of your children. They may say your hugs and kisses are mushy, but it will reinforce in their minds that sex and agape love belong together in the home where people are committed to one another for life.

Identification

In our day of unisex clothes and hairstyles, many more men dress like women and more women dress like men. Even worse, men are acting like women while women are acting like men. Dubious heros such as Michael Jackson and Boy George (usually with the name George you wouldn't need to point out it's a boy) have encouraged young people to shelve sexual differences. It concerns me that many Christian parents do not see the serious consequences of gender jumping.

God's Word warns against disregarding or confusing sexual differences: "A woman must not wear men's clothing, nor a man wear women's clothing, for the LORD your God detests anyone who does this" (Deut. 22:5). Even though both men and women of ancient Israel wore long robes, their dress was distinctive enough to indicate their gender.

This is not simply a cultural command. Consider Paul's admonition to believers at Corinth: "Does not the very nature of things teach you that if a man has long hair, it is a disgrace to him, but that if a woman has long hair, it is her glory?" (1 Cor. 11:14–15). As I understand Paul's words, a woman should enjoy or glory in the characteristics that set her apart from a man. The same principle applies to men.

Our sons are to identify with their dads and be proud they are growing up to be men—men of God. Our daughters should walk in the steps of their mothers, excited about becoming godly women, wives, and mothers. How does this happen? By positively reinforcing behavior that accentuates a child's masculinity or femininity. A boy's desire to be strong and protective ought to be encouraged. A girl who demonstrates inner beauty and a quiet and gentle spirit ought to be commended (1 Pet. 3:4).

Attitudes

While cultivating gender distinctives, we must be careful to guard our attitudes. Children, especially young children, learn more from our attitudes than they do from our words. They absorb what they sense more than what we say. Child psychiatrist Dr. Grace Ketterman stresses the critical relationship between acceptance, identification, and attitude:

Accept your child and love him exactly as he is. If your attitudes favor boys over girls (or vice versa) it will hurt your daughter and may give your son a superiority complex that may hurt him, too. It is tempting to cling to a dream you've always had of a certain kind of child—a great basketball player or a champion swimmer. As your child grows, it may be that he will exceed your dreams. But it often happens that he is too short for basketball or is afraid of water. Can you turn off your dream and sincerely love and approve of your child as he is? If your attitude toward him is one of disappointment, he will sense it. Furthermore, he will believe that he, not you, has failed and may give up or perhaps retaliate by hurting you in some way. I've worked with hundreds of rebellious young people. I have rarely seen one who was not emotionally hurt by his own parents. Unconditional acceptance is a prime factor in self-esteem, and that is essential to the future well-being of your child.[2]

What kind of attitude do you have toward the opposite sex? Whatever it is, it comes through loud and clear.

Modeling

Remember the well-worn phrase, "What you see is what you get"? I would like to change that to "What you see is what you do." The child that sees a healthy, happy, heterosexual relationship between Mom and Dad will be marked by this for life. The pattern will be branded on his heart and mind. Hard as he may try, he will not escape the memory of Mom and Dad openly embracing in his presence.

Our children will remember the way we talked to our mate and how we handled the difficult times together. In the archives of their minds, they will see us on our knees, together expressing our love for God and our appreciation for each other. To them, our model is and will forever remain the most powerful expression of our message.

But what if your model is not the best? Maybe your marriage needs an overhaul. Maybe you are parenting solo. No matter. You can still expose your child to other effective role models at church or even in your neighborhood.

We had contrasting models in two couples who were neighbors. One set of neighbors was a non-Christian couple who fought constantly. At one o'clock in the morning my family would be awakened by their fits of rage. Several times the police came to calm the chaos. One night the wife came to Teri and me for help after her husband had beaten her up. As we listened, I saw two wide-eyed children peeking around the corner wondering what was going on.

The next day they dumped buckets of questions about what had happened. I repeatedly pointed out that this couple did not know Jesus; they were both living for themselves rather than living to serve the Lord. I also drew a contrast they will remember for years to come. I talked about our other neighbors, a loving Christian couple with two small children. These dear friends communicated a deep love for each other and an uncompromising commitment to the Lord. They showered their children and ours with love and affection because they had faith in Jesus Christ and wanted to live for Him.

Conversations

Our actions speak louder than our words. But words effectively used will impart important information. So when talking to your child about sex, keep several guidelines in mind.

Be relaxed. I've talked about this before, but it's worth mentioning again. Whenever you talk about sex with your child, take a deep breath and exhale your anxiety. If you don't relax, your nervousness will be interpreted as either ignorance or fear.

Be prepared. Anticipate some of the questions your child will ask. They want to know where babies come from, how a baby gets in the mother's womb, and how the doctor gets the baby out. Think through how you will respond to these and other questions.

Fortunately, my wife was ready when our son at age seven asked, "What's AIDS?" She couched her answer in biblical truth, explaining that AIDS is a disease people get, usually because they don't use their bodies the way God intended.

One mother told me of a time her son caught her off guard by a very perceptive question:

> We had an unwed mother in our circle of friends. She was staying with neighbors during her pregnancy. I guess this piqued the curiosity of my two boys. We were discussing following God's plan and I was trying to explain to them that if you followed God's plan, you

wouldn't have children before you were married. One boy thought for a moment and said, "Oh, you mean if we do something bad, God might make us get pregnant?"

How would you have answered that question? Children have a remarkable ability to ask profound questions.

Be understanding. Not just older children but younger ones as well have a great deal of concern about their sexuality. When your little boy has an erection and turns away to hide it from you, don't just ignore it. Tell him it's normal and nothing to be concerned about. If you're his father, let him know that you have them too and that they sometimes embarrass you. This will help keep him from feeling strange or self-conscious.

If you're a mom and your little girl looks with curiosity at your breasts, explain to her the beautiful way God made a woman and how one day she'll have breasts like yours.

Be accurate. Always refer to the parts of the body using correct terminology. Doing anything less undermines the sanctity of our sexuality, gives a negative impression to our children, and may also come back to haunt you.

I have a friend who taught his two-and-a-half-year-old daughter to call a penis a "ding dong." He was slightly embarrassed when she asked her maternal grandfather if he had a ding dong like Daddy's.

A grandmother who took her grandson to go "potty" referred to his penis as a "tallywagger." Later the little boy said to his mom, "Guess what? Grandma thinks a penis is a tally-something!"

Be biblical. Use the Bible to answer questions concerning God's design for sex. Make sure you have a Bible appropriate for your child's age. Then read and refer to it when teaching about sex.

If we teach our children just one lesson in life, it should be to look to God and His Word to direct their lives. That's why my wife and I try to use the Bible as a handbook for teaching our children about sex.

WHAT SHOULD YOU TEACH YOUR CHILD?

When parents ask about how to teach children about sex, they typically have in mind the physical facts concerning reproduction.

They want to know how to comfortably describe male and female genitalia, as well as the actual act of intercourse.

For Christian parents, communicating about sex means far more than anatomy and reproduction. It represents an opportunity to teach children that their sexuality can best be understood and enjoyed when they look to God as the authority. So in the early years, you should make a strong, positive association between sexuality and the Scriptures. The seeds you plant in your children's younger years will eventually germinate and bring forth the fruit of a biblically based sexual relationship in their adult years.

The Bible Tells You Who You Are

Several years ago, I was asked to speak to a parent-teacher group from a local public school. More than one hundred prominent Dallasites, both Christians and non-Christians, met in the school cafeteria. I spoke on the four pillars of parenting. The first pillar I described was the pillar of purpose. My contention was that if we don't know our purpose in life, we can't possibly give sound direction to our children.

Then I asked them, "Why are you alive, and where are you going?"

My words were met with blank stares. There was an eerie silence of conviction. Even the social and economic kingpins were literally bowled over with a simple question of purpose.

How would you answer that same question? Do you know why you are alive and where you are going? If not, how can you lead your children?

The Westminster Confession of Faith gives one of the best statements of purpose ever developed. "The chief end of man is to know God and to enjoy Him forever." Let me put a parental twist on it. "The chief end of a child is to know God and enjoy Him forever." Even children in diapers have a purpose in life, and we as their parents must communicate that purpose.

Impress upon your children the life lesson of Ephesians 2:8–10: "I mean that you are saved by grace, and you got that grace by believing. You did not save yourselves. It was a gift from God. God has made us what we are. In Christ Jesus, God made us new people so that we would do good works. God had planned in advance those good works for us. He had planned for us to live our lives doing them" (ICB).

These simple verses map out God's plan for a full and abundant life. First, we have to place our trust in Jesus Christ or pay the penalty for our sins. Second, we can never be good enough or work hard enough to pay for our sins. And finally, once we trust Jesus to forgive us, we have His mission to accomplish while we are here on earth. *His* plan becomes *our* purpose.

God Used Mom's and Dad's Bodies to Create Your Body

When it comes time to explain reproduction to your child, do so in a biblical context. Turn to Genesis chapter two and read verses 18–25.

> Then the Lord God said, "It is not good for the man to be alone. I will make a helper who is right for him."
>
> From the ground God formed every wild animal and every bird in the sky. He brought them to the man so the man could name them. Whatever the man called each living thing, that became its name. The man gave names to all the tame animals, to the birds in the sky and to all the wild animals.
>
> But Adam did not find a helper that was right for him. So the Lord God caused the man to sleep very deeply. While the man was asleep, God took one of the ribs from the man's body. Then God closed the man's skin at the place where he took the rib. The Lord God used the rib from the man to make a woman. Then the Lord brought the woman to the man.
>
> And the man said,
>
> "Now this is someone whose bones came from my bones.
>
> Her body came from my body.
>
> I will call her 'woman,' because she was taken out of man."
>
> So a man will leave his father and mother and be united with his wife. And the two people will become one body.
>
> The man and his wife were naked, but they were not ashamed.
> (ICB)

Teach human sexuality from this passage. Even very young children will understand the following observations drawn from this text:

- God made a man, but the man was lonely and needed someone with whom to share his life.
- God made a woman who could be a wife for the man.
- God planned for them to be together so they could have children.
- God made the man with a penis and the woman with a vagina and womb so the man could be a dad and the woman a mom.
- God told them to join their bodies together in a very special way to show their love for each other and to have babies.

As your child matures, explain how husband and wife join their bodies together. Regardless of how much you describe, make sure to put it in the framework of the Bible and God's command to be fruitful.

After teaching your child the facts from this passage, make the application to your own situation. You can speak in more general terms or get specific, as I have below:

> *God made you by having Mom and Dad share our bodies just like Adam and Eve. God used sperm from Dad's body and joined it with an egg from Mom's body, and together the egg and sperm formed you. At that moment you started to grow, and God knew that you would be a boy (girl). So you are very special to God and to us because God used our bodies to give you life.*

God Formed You in Your Mom's Womb

As sexual union is viewed as part of God's creation, build on your child's understanding of sex, as well as her self-esteem, by explaining how she was fashioned by God in her mother's womb.

Read King David's words and let your voice express the heart of the psalmist as he cried out to God:

> You made my whole being.
> You formed me in my mother's body.
> I praise you because you made me in an amazing and
> wonderful way.
> What you have done is wonderful.
> I know this very well.   (Ps. 139:13–14; ICB)

What a wealth of information for our children! Make sure you capture the text's beauty and majesty as you explain it to your child:

> *Although God used Mom's and Dad's bodies, God was the one who created you and caused you to grow in Mom's womb. Even before you were born, God knew and loved you. You are a wonderful creation of God.*

Continue using this passage as a springboard to tell your child about the miracle of life:

> *Let me tell you how God made you. Out of millions and millions of sperm, He took just one and joined it with an egg inside your mom. He chose which sperm and which egg to bring together, in order to create you. When the sperm and egg came together, you were conceived, which means your life began. But God didn't stop there. He then watched as you grew in Mom's womb. He made you a girl (boy) and chose the color of your eyes and hair. Because He made you, you can say the same thing King David said, "I am fearfully and wonderfully made."*

What a tremendous dose of biblical self-esteem mixed with a positive presentation of sexual union and reproduction!

NOVA has produced a video for public television entitled "The Miracle of Life." It shows how out of millions of sperm only one is able to penetrate and fertilize the egg. Although there are several plugs for the theory of macro-evolution, this film captures the wonders of reproduction and serves as a great tool for teaching your child how God fashioned him or her in the womb.

You Are a Gift from God

"You are a product of our love for one another." What a message to convey to our children. They are not accidents. They are gifts from God that reflect the love moms and dads have for each other.

Reassure your children of your love by drawing a parallel between your desire to have them and Hannah's and Elkanah's desire to have a child. Explain how this couple wanted to have children and could not. Read the account that tells how Hannah was deeply troubled because she could not have a baby. With tears in her eyes, she prayed to God to give her a child. Hannah and her husband also prayed together for a baby. Then they had intercourse and God allowed a baby to grow in Hannah's womb (1 Sam. 1:12–20). The sequence of longing for a child, praying, having intercourse, and receiving a baby illustrates God's hand at work in the union of a married couple.

Then apply Hannah and Elkanah's story to your own experience:

Dad and I wanted to have a baby just as Hannah and Elkanah did. We prayed for a baby just as they did. After we prayed and shared our love for each other, you started to grow inside my womb. When you were born, Dad and I thanked God for you. You are a very special gift from Him.

Shortly after our children were born, Teri used her calligraphy skills to make a copy of Hannah's praise to God for giving her Samuel. Above the bed in each of our children's rooms is a print that reads: "I prayed for this child and the LORD has granted me what I asked of Him. So now I give him to the LORD. For his whole life he will be given over to the LORD" (1 Sam. 1:27–28).

Children are a gift from the Lord and should know that's exactly how we view them. If they don't hear it from us, don't expect them to hear it from anyone else.

God Doesn't Want You to Use Bad Words

Many young children are barraged with filthy language from their peers. Tragically, slang terminology for parts of the body and for sexual intercourse can demean God's good gift. To build dignity and self-respect, we must counter the gutter language our kids will hear. One passage especially helpful in this regard is Ephesians 4:29: "When you talk, do not say harmful things. But say what people need—words that will help others become stronger. Then what you say will help those who listen to you" (ICB).

The word *harmful* means unwholesome, bad, or worthless. Certain kinds of words or talk are harmful because they make something God made to be good seem bad.

A few verses later Paul places harmful talk in the context of sexual immorality: "But there must be no sexual sin among you. There must not be any kind of evil or greed. Those things are not right for God's holy people. Also, there must be no evil talk among you. You must not speak foolishly or tell evil jokes. These things are not right for you. But you should be giving thanks to God" (Eph. 5:3–4; ICB).

In this passage we are told that our behavior should be so pure that no one would even suspect us of immorality. In addition, our language should reflect our purity. Any words that do not express a proper view of sex are out of place for the Christian.

So how does all this apply to a Christian child? He should know that there are people who use unwholesome or harmful words. People who use these words do not appreciate the way God made us. Tell your child God expects us to only use words that help people to know and love God. Bad words won't do that.

Your Body Is Special

If children learn to respect their bodies, this lesson could translate into a healthy fear of sexually transmitted diseases.

My children have suffered with allergy problems, which they inherited from dear old Dad. The symptoms range from respiratory problems to mood swings. Their problems became so severe that we had to find a solution or a mental hospital for Mom and Dad. We found a solution, and for us it happened to be nutrition. When as a family we started eating better foods and took vitamins to supplement apparent deficiencies, our children's health and behavior changed dramatically.

I share this experience not to sell you "Nieder's Notes on Nutrition," but to point out that out of our dietary disciplines our children developed a growing respect for their bodies along with a great deal of self-control. When my son was six and complaining about all the candy bars he had missed out on, I told him that one day soon I would let him eat anything he wanted for an entire day. Then I asked, "How much would you eat?"

He said, "I wouldn't eat too much because I would just get sick and mess up my body."

Teri had to pick me up off the floor. We were both amazed that he had caught our concern for good health.

The Old Testament story of Daniel, Hananiah, Mishael, and Azariah illustrates what a proper diet can do for a young person. All four were taken into captivity in Babylon and were chosen by the king to eat from the royal table and be educated in the language and literature of Babylon. In order to keep the Jewish law, Daniel asked if he and his friends could eat vegetables or grain rather than the rich food and wine from the king's table. The guard reluctantly agreed to a ten-day trial run. At the end of the period, Daniel and his friends "looked healthier and better nourished than any of the young men who ate the royal food" (Dan. 1:15).

Some commentators feel that their healthier appearance was because God miraculously blessed these young men for their obedience. But I think the connection between the food and the appearance is cause and effect. (You are what you eat.) Even if this is not the case, there is an obvious message here. These young men in their late teens or early twenties respected their bodies and themselves enough to honor God, even in what they ate. That's a message our children need to hear, especially with AIDS and sexually transmitted diseases running rampant.

PASSING THE TORCH OF TRUTH

Parents preparing young children would do well to also remember Timothy. When he was a little boy, his unbelieving dad was probably apathetic and at times angry about his mother's faith. For years his mother and grandmother took turns setting Timothy on their laps and reading the sacred writings to him. As a teenager, he developed a reputation for being a person of integrity and commitment. Years later, when Timothy was serving as pastor of a difficult church, Paul reminded him of those who had taught him the Word. When Timothy looked back, he saw the solid foundation upon which he had built his life and ministry, and he pressed on, even in the face of adversity.

When our children become teenagers, young adults, and parents, what will they see when they look back? As they look back through the tunnel of time, will they see Mom and Dad teaching them the sacred writings?

The water main in front of our house has broken at least a dozen times. After fixing the latest leak, the street crew patched up the street with cement. One day all the members of our family wrote their names in the cement while it was still drying. Years later, despite traffic and the weather, our names remained.

Young children are like wet cement. The impressions we make on them will be there for years to come. Nothing will be able to erase them. Nothing. What marks are you etching in the wet cement of your child's life?

GIVE IT SOME THOUGHT

1. Does your child understand God's role in creating the sexes?

2. Does your child view his or her sexuality as a product of God's handiwork?

3. Does your child see and experience open expressions of love and affection in your home?

4. Is your child developing a healthy identity with a parent of the same sex?

5. What kind of a model does your child see in your home? What improvements do you think you should make?

6. Are you anticipating your child's questions and looking for teachable moments? How can you do better at this?

7. Does your child view himself or herself as a precious gift from God? If not, why?

CHAPTER 11

Masturbation

No other area of sexuality induces such strong feelings and opinions as masturbation. For some, the subject provokes widespread guilt, while others consider it a healthy form of sexual expression. Even respected Bible teachers cannot agree. One calls it sin while another views it as God's gift to the single person. Most doctors, psychologists, and other professionals feel that masturbation is normal and harmless and occurs naturally during the developing adolescent years.

With a broad spectrum of leaders holding divergent views, many people are confused and concerned. Christian parents who want to communicate a biblical view of masturbation feel like pawns in the middle of a debate.

Why is there such debate on this issue? Because the Scriptures do not directly condone or condemn masturbation. In fact, there are no specific references to masturbation in the Scriptures. Does that mean we can do what we want? No way. As with many other behaviors not directly addressed in the Bible, we still must apply biblical principles to determine their appropriateness. But if we determine that masturbation is not acceptable, can we impose our perception on our child? Obviously not. Masturbation is a young person's choice—a choice parents cannot control. Since we cannot govern his or her behavior even if we want to and there are no biblical commands against it, masturbation should be a young person's decision. Certainly a decision that should be based on biblical and practical considerations and the leading of the Holy Spirit. But it's his or her decision—not ours.

Discussing masturbation presents several instructional opportunities. We can show a child how to consult God's Word when a subject is not directly addressed in the Scriptures. We can also demonstrate how to secondarily weigh practical concerns when the Bible does not make a definitive statement. Furthermore, we can use it to teach a child to listen to the inner promptings of the Holy Spirit.

Although the decision to masturbate is one we cannot make for our children, it is one we can guide them in while we allow God to lead them.

WHAT DOES THE OLD TESTAMENT SAY?

Most Bible teachers agree that the Word of God does not make a direct statement about masturbation. But some suggest that the account of Onan in Genesis 38:9–11 gives us some insight. Onan's older brother, Er, died without fathering children. The continuation of one's family line meant so much to the people of that day that a cultural custom emerged in which the brother of the deceased had the obligation to produce offspring on behalf of his brother. Following the custom of the levirate marriage, Onan had intercourse with his brother's wife. But for selfish reasons, he withdrew at the moment of orgasm. "But Onan knew that the offspring would not be his; so whenever he lay with his brother's wife, he spilled his seed on the ground to keep from producing offspring for his brother. What he did was wicked in the LORD's sight, so he put him to death also."

Close inspection of this admittedly strange scenario shows that it does not refer to masturbation but to the interruption of sexual intercourse (coitus interruptus). God judged Onan for his self-centered reluctance to produce a child who would gain an inheritance before he did. Onan's sin had nothing to do with masturbation; it had everything to do with selfishness.

Of greater relevance are several Old Testament passages which discuss an emission of semen that could be the product of masturbation or a nocturnal emission (wet dream). In Leviticus 15:16–17, we read: "When a man has an emission of semen, he must bathe his whole body with water, and he will be unclean till evening. Any clothing or leather that has semen on it must be washed with water, and it will be unclean till evening."

In this passage (and others such as Leviticus 22:4 and Deuteronomy 23:10–11), we find that an emission of semen made a man "unclean" and therefore unable to participate in prescribed religious practices until certain restorative procedures were followed.

Our cultural orientation coupled with twentieth-century technology makes all of this seem rather strange. We find ourselves asking, what does it mean to be "unclean"? What's "unclean" about an emission of semen? We must understand that unclean meant to be unfit for certain religious practices. God established certain boundaries for the behavior of His people. Some boundaries were for their benefit and do not necessarily represent sinful behavior. For example, a woman was considered unclean during her menstrual cycle, which she obviously could not avoid and which was not a product of her sin. So why did God classify an emission of semen as unclean? Although we cannot be absolutely certain, several suggestions have merit.

First of all, cleansing procedures following an emission of semen may have had some hygienic purpose. In view of how AIDS spreads through body fluids such as semen, we cannot totally discount the hygienic validity of these practices.

Second, these regulations demonstrate that God wanted to be intimately involved in every aspect of the life of His people. He cares about what takes place even when no one else is around.

Third, these guidelines heightened personal sensitivity toward sexual behavior. They encouraged self-control and appropriate sexual restraint.

What then can we learn about masturbation from these Levitical practices? We cannot reach a conclusion as to its morality, especially since the emission of semen in these cases may not have been from masturbation. We can only observe that God wants to be involved in the most intimate aspects of our lives, including masturbation—a practice the Old Testament neither condones nor condemns.

WHAT DOES THE NEW TESTAMENT SAY?

As with the Old Testament, the New Testament does not make a direct statement about masturbation, although several passages shed light on the practice.

In 1 Corinthians 7:1–5, we read:

It is good for a man not to marry. But since there is so much immorality, each man should have his own wife, and each woman her own husband. The husband should fulfill his marital duty to his wife, and likewise the wife to her husband. In the same way, the husband's body does not belong to him alone but also to his wife. Do not deprive each other except by mutual consent and for a time, so that you may devote yourselves to prayer. Then come together again so that Satan will not tempt you because of your lack of self-control.

Without delving into the full meaning of this passage, let me make two observations relative to masturbation. The solution for "burn[ing] with passion" (v. 9) was a marriage relationship, not the sexual release that comes from masturbation. Keep in mind Paul's unmarried state when writing these words. Why didn't he include masturbation as a way to douse the fire of personal passion? He certainly knew about it. So why did he not mention it?

Moreover, the safeguard against immorality is not masturbation but the receptivity and availability of one's spouse. In fact, abstinence was to be only for a short time and by mutual consent with the defined purpose of prayer. The safeguard was marital union, not self-stimulation.

These observations deserve careful consideration even though they don't speak directly to the issue of masturbation.

Paul's first letter to the believers of Thessalonica contains another important passage: "It is God's will that you should be sanctified: that you should avoid sexual immorality; that each of you should learn to control his own body in a way that is holy and honorable, not in passionate lust like the heathen, who do not know God" (1 Thess. 4:3–5).

Learning how to control our own bodies helps us avoid sexual immorality. Paul's emphasis is on control, which may or may not include the temporary release of sexual pressure.

God considers our method for controlling our bodies to be important. We should control our bodies in a holy and honorable way. Holy means to set apart. To Christians, it carries the idea of being set apart to serve God. So a Christian's method of self-control is to be distinct and honorable to God. Distinct as compared to unbelievers who do not know God. Honorable in terms of personal dignity before God.

With this in mind, let's pose the obvious question: Can masturbation be considered a holy and honorable way to control our bodies and avoid sexual immorality?

Another important passage should weigh heavily in our consideration of masturbation. Jesus Christ condemned lust as a sin. His words are clear: "Anyone who looks at a woman lustfully has already committed adultery with her in his heart" (Matt. 5:28). Can masturbation occur apart from lustful fantasies? Can it be simply a biological release of pent-up sexual energies apart from sexual fantasy? Credible people hold different positions. I have counseled with a number of people and received letters from many more who struggle with masturbatory behavior. Almost without exception, they have fueled their passions by viewing sexually explicit material. When lust has had its way, the urgency of sexual release leads to masturbation.

The Scriptures do not directly state that masturbation can be used as a way to control our passions. Nor do they directly condemn the practice. How then can we arrive at a decision? How can we instruct our children?

When the Bible does not give us a direct command, we should carefully consider biblical principles that have immediate relevance. If God guides us in one direction or another through these principles, we need look no further. If the passages we have examined have led you to a decision, stop. You have found your answer. Now what you need to do is work the answer out in your life and that of your child.

On the other hand, if you are still uncertain, you should weigh practical considerations that God may use to shed additional light on the subject.

PRACTICAL CONSIDERATIONS

After studying the biblical evidence relative to masturbation, examine some practical issues relative to solo sex. These should never be given greater credence than the Bible, but they can be useful when the scriptural evidence is inconclusive. Once you and your child have carefully explored scriptural principles that relate to masturbation, work through a list of the positives and negatives of that practice.

The Pros

1. Masturbation allows children to learn about their bodies.
2. A person who masturbates can become more easily orgasmic in marriage.
3. Masturbation can release sexual energy and thus reduce the temptation to engage in premarital or extramarital intercourse.

The Cons

1. Masturbation may lead to a self-centered sexual identity, while the Bible stresses mutual satisfaction.
2. Instant gratification can decrease self-control, which may lessen the enjoyment of sex in marriage because of premature ejaculation by the man.
3. Masturbation may fuel excessive and unhealthy sexual fantasies.
4. The magnetic power of sex that brings a married couple together can be diminished rather than heightened by masturbation.

MASTURBATION AND YOUNG CHILDREN

A child will naturally explore his own body. If you find your young child masturbating, don't ignore it and don't condemn it. Take the opportunity to communicate your love, acceptance, and understanding and the wonders of the human body as God created it. You might put them this way:

> *It feels good to touch your body's private areas, doesn't it? God made you that way. As you get older, you will understand why. Your body happens to be a magnificent machine that God designed for you to use in order to work for Him. Because our bodies are special to God, we should take care of them.*

There are times when a child's masturbatory behavior can become excessive or inappropriate. Some parents fear they will negatively mark their child if they demand the behavior be controlled. But the fear is unwarranted if we have a relaxed, positive attitude.

Simply saying "I know it feels good, but now is not the time" will work in most cases.

MASTURBATION IN THE ADOLESCENT AND TEEN YEARS

During puberty, masturbation becomes a greater concern since it is a response to new and growing sexual desires. While being very sensitive to your child's feelings, initiate a conversation about masturbation before you suspect such behavior. Your child needs to hear about masturbation from you—not from his friends. And since an estimated 98 percent of men and 80 percent of women have reportedly masturbated, you can be confident that this will be a concern for your adolescent or teen. So you must talk to your child about it: How?

A dad could say to his son:

> *Son, you may find it hard to believe but I know the intense sexual desires you now have. I have been there; I do know what you are going through. Now I realize that you have heard the other kids talking about "playing with themselves." The correct word for this is masturbation. It refers to massaging your penis in such a way that it causes you to release semen.*
>
> *Now as a Christian, you really need to know how the Lord wants you to control your sexual desires. Some people feel masturbation is wrong, and others think it's fine. I want to show you what God says. God knows how tough it is for you to control your desires. But know that He will help you to control them. Let's look at some verses in the Old and New Testaments that you probably have never read before. After we study these passages, ask the Holy Spirit what He wants you to do. He wants to guide you so that whatever you do will bring honor to Jesus Christ.*

Helping your adolescent or teen to decide how God feels about masturbation will not be a once and done conversation. Gauge your content and conversation to your child's age and growing sexual desires. Remember what you hope to accomplish in taking this approach. You want your child to:

- Understand God's desire to be involved in his sexuality;
- Directly look to God's Word for direction;
- Experience God's and your unconditional love and acceptance of him;
- Become sensitive to the leading of the Holy Spirit;
- See the relevancy and application of the Scriptures to his life.

As you work through this "process" with your child, it will reap spiritual and relational dividends and will place masturbation in a proper perspective.

A CLOSING CONCERN

The topic of masturbation may very well be the most difficult to address with your child because it is intensely personal. But he needs to talk about it, and he needs to discuss it with you, not his confused peers. If you don't talk about it with him, he could suffer a serious spiritual or emotional setback. One man shared with me the confusion and despair that resulted from his childhood ignorance on this topic:

> What happened in my life started when I was in the fifth grade, ten years old. I started masturbating to be accepted with the other boys at the grade school I attended. I was not sexually mature enough for that then. As a result I had a double rupture (where the testicles ascend to their position before birth). It scared me. I did not know anything about the birds and the bees. I didn't tell anyone, not even my parents. I would hear my dad joke around with other guys when they almost got hit in the nuts and say, "Boy, a little closer and you would have sung high soprano in the choir." When I heard that, I thought I was going to turn into a girl! I stopped masturbating, hoping that the ruptures would heal. They didn't and this compounded my fears. To make a long story short, I accepted the idea that I was going to turn into a girl, so I started looking at girls with more curiosity. I wanted to be a girl. I was headed toward a gay lifestyle and didn't even know it.

This letter represents others I have received from individuals who were traumatized as children because of ignorance. Don't let it happen to your child.

There is a form of masturbatory behavior that I was ignorant of until I read a letter from a courageous mother who wanted to alert parents. What happened to her son further demonstrates the need to talk openly and honestly with our children.

My fifteen-year-old son died of autoerotic asphyxia earlier this year. I am writing this in the hope that it may save some young person's life in your community.

The coroner's report read: "Death by accidental hanging— autoerotic asphyxia." We didn't even know what that meant, but we soon found out. A-A, which began as a cult practice, has been going on since the early 1900s. This potentially deadly practice is a means of getting a sexual high by masturbating while controlling the flow of blood to the brain with a rope, plastic bag, or shoestring.

Many young people are not aware that engaging in this practice can cost them their lives. Over one thousand young lives are claimed yearly. Because parents would rather have people believe their children died of suicide, the statistics have been kept quiet. As parents, you should talk to your children and warn them of the dangers of this practice. You may be able to prevent an unnecessary death.

Look for pornographic materials in their rooms. Be suspicious of knotted T-shirts or plastic bags. Be concerned if your child comes out of his room with bloodshot eyes or red marks around his neck or if he seems disoriented.

I hope and pray that no other family has to suffer the pain I am going through because of this deadly practice.

I too hope and pray that no young person or family has to suffer the consequences of sexual ignorance.

Talking about masturbation won't be easy, but it's necessary, even critical. Once you get beyond the initial discomfort, you and your child will be bonded together in a profound intimacy.

GIVE IT SOME THOUGHT

1. How do you suspect your child's friends will present masturbation?

2. Are you prepared to respond if you inadvertently discover your child masturbating?

3. Do you think your child already knows about masturbation? What does he or she know?

4. Can you anticipate a good time to discuss masturbation with your child?

5. Does your child know about autoerotic asphyxia? Do you have any indications that he could be engaged in this deadly practice?

CHAPTER 12

Homosexuality

"If I ever catch you hitchhiking, it will be the last thing you ever do!" Those haunting words came from the lips of my dear mother, who always knew how to communicate her convictions.

Despite repeated warnings, one afternoon as I grew impatient waiting for a bus, I accepted a ride from a man who interpreted my dangling hand as an appeal for a ride.

Less than a minute after I got into the car, the man asked if I hitchhiked much. With my fifteen-year-old masculinity at stake, I lied and said, "Yes."

He asked, "Have you ever been picked up by a fag before?"

Fear bolted through my body. For a moment I thought I heard my mother shouting, "I told you never to hitchhike!" I clenched my fist and decided if he came near me, I would punch him, throw open the door, and jump. Since we were going about thirty-five miles an hour, it would have been interesting!

Rather than appear naive and vulnerable, I boldly told him yes (another lie).

Using gutter terms, he asked if I allowed this other homosexual to perform a sex act on me.

With my heart and mind racing, I said, "No, but—I beat him up, and later my father killed him." Then I screamed, "Pull over and let me out or you're next."

Now fear bolted through *his* body. He quickly pulled over and let me out.

On the highway called life, our children are being invited to hitchhike with the wrong lifestyle. Homosexuality has been granted the status of acceptability, largely due to the impact of the "gay liberation" movement begun in the seventies.

Parents are concerned and rightly so. The militant homosexual agenda undermines the family. One researcher lists fifteen goals and objectives of the gay liberation movement. Here are some of the highlights:

- Homosexuals should be permitted to be gay any place, any time.
- Government taxes should be used to perform free change of sex operations on homosexuals whenever they are demanded.
- Children should be taught in school about all kinds of human sexuality. Children should not be told that one mode of satisfying one's sexual needs is healthier, more normal, or better than any other.
- All organized religions should be condemned for helping in the genocide of homosexuals.
- The family as we now know it should be abolished.
- Homosexuals should be placed in positions as caregivers and permitted to become teachers, clergy, counselors, therapists, and social workers. They should be allowed to participate in the rearing and education of children.
- There should be a repeal of all laws against sodomy, homosexuality, pederasty, sadomasochism, and any other form of sexual behavior between consenting adults done in private.
- Homosexuality should be taught as one of the ways of birth control and population control.
- Society should prohibit the rearing of girls as girls and boys as boys and foster a kind of unisex role for all children.
- There should be the development of sexual utopias composed of separate neighborhoods, some for women only and some for men only, so that homosexuals can reach full identity and feel completely at ease.[1]

Not every homosexual would endorse these goals and objectives, but militant homosexuals tend to direct the movement.

The following prose, while extreme, reveals the mindset of some radical homosexuals. In the February 15, 1987, issue of the *Gay Community News of Boston,* Michael Swift's "For the Homoerotic Order" was published.

We shall sodomize your sons, emblems of your feeble masculinity, of your shallow dreams and vulgar lies. We shall seduce them in your schools, in your dormitories, in your gymnasiums, in your locker rooms, in your sports arenas, in your seminaries, in your youth groups, in your movie theater bathrooms, in your army bunkhouses, in your truck stops, in your all-male clubs, in your houses of congress, wherever men are with men together. Your sons shall become our minions and do our bidding. They will be recast in our image. They will come to crave and adore us . . . .

The family unit—spawning ground of lies, betrayals, mediocrity, hypocrisy, and violence will be abolished. The family unit, which only dampens imagination and curbs free will, must be eliminated.

Perfect boys will be conceived and grown in the genetic laboratory. They will be bonded together in communal settings, under the control and instruction of homosexual savants.

All churches who condemn us will be closed. Our only gods are handsome young men. We adhere to a cult of beauty, moral and esthetic. All that is ugly and vulgar and banal will be annihilated. . . .

We are fueled with ferocious bitterness . . . . We too are capable of firing guns and manning the barricades of the ultimate revolution.

Tremble, hetero swine, when we appear before you without our masks.[2]

Swift's words are frightening and reminiscent of those who lived in the ancient cities of Sodom and Gomorrah. They, too, demanded sexual access to anyone who entered their cities.

WHAT CAUSES HOMOSEXUALITY?

In the wake of the gay liberation movement, several diverse theories have attempted to define and defend homosexuality.

Is There a Biological Basis?

Does God make a person homosexual, or does a person decide to become a homosexual? Is there a biological or environmental cause of homosexual behavior?

A biological basis for homosexuality would be either a genetic trait or a chemical imbalance. But neither option has received support from the medical establishment. Dr. William P. Wilson states:

The experience of many therapists and investigators strongly implicates disturbed parental relationships with the child and significant others in the nurturing environment as well as between the significant others themselves. I use the term *significant others* because I have found that grandparents, uncles, aunts, cousins, and siblings can be involved. There is, then, good evidence that psychological factors play a significant role in determining their aberrant psychosexual-object choice and sexual orientation. There is no substantial evidence at the present to show that genetic or hormonal factors play a direct or indirect role in the development of homosexuality.[3]

Even if someone were predisposed to a homosexual lifestyle, it would not make the behavior acceptable. Do chronic headaches or PMS (premenstrual syndrome) give a person the license to engage in socially unacceptable behavior? If a person was found to be predisposed to anger, would we then conclude that it was okay for him to rage out of control? No. So even if we discovered a biological tendency toward homosexuality, it would still not make the behavior morally or socially acceptable.

Is There an Environmental Basis?

Since it is doubtful that biology plays a role in homosexual behavior, researchers and homosexual advocates have looked for other causative factors. Various psychological theories have been proposed. From the psychoanalytic camp comes the suggestion that homosexuality stems from a person's being developmentally locked at a homosexual phase most other people pass through. Behaviorism, in contrast, offers an environmental view. Behaviorists claim that homosexuality is learned behavior which results from a homosexual encounter. A fourteen-year-old high school boy at camp who is seduced by a male counselor and experiences the intense pleasure of an orgasm may opt for a homosexual lifestyle as a consequence.

While circumstances may help establish the sexual pattern, the primary determinant is a person's choice.

WHAT IS HOMOSEXUALITY?

Dr. George A. Rekers, in his excellent book *Growing Up Straight: What Every Family Should Know about Homosexuality,* defines homosexuality in terms of sexual behavior, lust, and temptation. Rekers states that homosexual behavior is "the physical contact between two or more persons of the same sex, recognized by each as a sexual contact and usually resulting in physiological sexual arousal. There are many different types of such physical contact, but all are instances of homosexual behavior whether or not sexual climax results."[4]

Dr. Rekers defines homosexual lust as thinking about a sexual encounter with a member of one's own sex. The thoughts may or may not cause physiological arousal. He further states: "All homosexual lust is abnormal and fights against normal sexual adjustment. Each instance of homosexual lust conditions the nervous system to an ever stronger responsiveness to homosexual stimulation."[5] He goes on to stress that the first step toward a homosexual orientation is the temptation to engage in homosexual lust, which leads to homosexual behavior. Although abnormal and certainly not desirable, the temptation in itself is not sinful.

WHAT'S A PARENT TO DO?

Parents should have several goals in teaching their children about homosexuality. We must begin with the goal of protecting our kids from being solicited by a homosexual. Many homosexuals adopted their lifestyle because they were either recruited or seduced as teenagers or preteens.

Our second goal must be to explain what God says about heterosexuality and homosexuality. Our children are going to be confronted with homosexuality as a sexual option. So it's essential that a positive biblical view of heterosexuality be taught before a young person has to deal with the issue of homosexuality. We need to teach what is right before explaining what is wrong.

Then we must communicate that certain affections for members of the same sex do not make one a homosexual. Homosexuals solicit young people with the lie that any affection for members of the same sex indicates a homosexual orientation. We cannot allow this lie to be perpetrated on naive, unsuspecting children.

Protecting Preadolescent Children

Does a young child need to know about homosexuality? Will such knowledge help protect him or her from AIDS or from being solicited? Won't a child be stripped of innocence and security when confronted with the unnatural moral option of homosexuality? Could he be confused to the point where he would define his feelings for a member of the same sex as homosexuality when in fact the affection has nothing to do with sexual attraction?

If a younger child has been properly schooled in self-protection, he does not need explicit information regarding homosexuality and homosexual practices. The umbrella of protection from all forms of sexual abuse should be sufficient to warn our children that they are prey for molesters. Describing what these people might do to them in terms of heterosexual or homosexual activity would create unwarranted fears and incredible stress.

The key in the early years is your careful consideration of situations where your child might be at risk. Baby sitters must be screened. Other homes in the neighborhood should be off limits until you can be confident of your child's security.

While protecting your children, we also need to prepare them for a Sodom-and-Gomorrah-like society. There's plenty we can do even in the younger years, but it won't be easy. Helping a child deal with the moral mess of homosexuality is like trying to get a ten-year-old to drive an eighteen-wheel truck.

Constantly reinforce heterosexuality and monogamy as God's plan for the family. The opening chapters of Genesis give us the prototype. God created a man and a woman for sexual union within marriage. He did not create people to engage in homosexual relationships. The rest of the Scriptures bear out this fact.

With your young child, take every opportunity to point to healthy, heterosexual couples such as Abraham and Sarah, Isaac and Rebekah, Zechariah and Elizabeth. These were men and women who became husband and wife in order to have families. You can reinforce this simple truth with the geneologies, or family trees, found throughout the Word of God.

Explain that some people disobey God. When your child sees homosexuals embracing or kissing, describe them as people who are not following God's plan for their lives. Label their behavior as wrong. If your child wants more information, focus on God's perfect plan of heterosexual monogamy.

Teach with godly models of heterosexual monogamy. Looking

back over years of counseling, Dr. Howard Hendricks said, "I have never seen a homosexual come from a home where both the mother and father were incurably in love with Jesus Christ and with each other." The model of a God-fearing, heterosexual couple is the best safeguard against homosexual tendencies.

If you're a single parent, don't panic. Instead, build a supportive relationship with some couples in the church you attend. Just one couple or even a godly man or woman with an interest in your child can counter much of the potentially negative impact of an absent dad or mom.

Encourage sex-role differentiation. In a society that promotes unisex behavior by feminizing men and masculinizing women, this will become increasingly more difficult. We are becoming jaded by the gender blending of our world. The cure is to teach your son to be proud of his masculinity and to look forward to the prospect of being a husband and a father. Also teach your daughter to be proud of her femininity, mindful that one day she may get married and have her body bring forth new life.

Teaching Teens about Homosexuality

Whenever she tells the story, her voice cracks with emotion. While walking up a stairwell in her school, my wife, Teri, then just eighteen years old, was cornered by a lesbian. Though startled and frightened, she was still able to break away from this girl's grasp.

Homosexuals have become increasingly aggressive in their pursuit of "converts." Since homosexuals cannot biologically reproduce themselves, they frequently solicit young people to fulfill their abhorrent purposes.

In order to deal adequately with this phenomenon, we must seek out God's written counsel. And as we do, we must be very sensitive to our children's struggle during puberty. Rapid physical growth and new desires are seeds of an identity crisis—seeds that could grow in either a heterosexual or a homosexual direction. Nothing could be more important (or more difficult) than to keep the relational door open with our children during these tumultuous years. To do so, we must accept our children's sexuality while openly and honestly communicating our love and God's plan for them.

WHAT GOD SAYS ABOUT HOMOSEXUALITY

Proponents of the homosexual lifestyle include professing Christians who teach that God does not condemn homosexual sex. In an attempt to build a biblical defense of their sexuality, they have developed intricate yet distorted arguments to counter the clear teaching of the Word of God. To bolster their credibility, they have even turned to the original languages of the Bible to support their claims.

While some try to twist the truth, others simply dismiss what the Bible teaches as being cultural and irrelevant. They deny moral absolutes and in effect treat the Bible as merely another book.

If you have not studied the relevant passages on homosexuality, you can be sold a bill of goods and walk away thinking that homosexuality is not wrong. Nothing could be further from the truth. Homosexual behavior and homosexual lust are sins, sins which God can and will forgive—but sins nonetheless. And because they are not only immoral but also unnatural, they are particularly devastating.

Homosexuality Incurs God's Judgment

In Genesis 19 we have the familiar account of Sodom and Gomorrah. Homosexuality was running rampant. When two angels met Lot at the entrance to the cities, Lot invited them to his house rather than expose them to the aggressive homosexuals who roamed the city streets. They finally agreed to spend the night at Lot's home. After dinner Lot's house came under siege.

> Before they had gone to bed, all the men from every part of the city of Sodom—both young and old—surrounded the house. They called to Lot, "Where are the men who came to you tonight? Bring them out to us so that we can have sex with them."
>
> Lot went outside to meet them and shut the door behind him and said, "No, my friends. Don't do this wicked thing. Look, I have two daughters who have never slept with a man. Let me bring them out to you, and you can do what you like with them. But don't do anything to these men, for they have come under the protection of my roof" (vv. 4–8).

These men perceived the angels as men and wanted to have sex with them. When Lot offered them his daughters, they said no.

Advocates of homosexuality attempt to teach that the men of the city did not want to have sex but simply wanted to show hospitality to the strangers. They claim that the Hebrew word *yada,* which means to know and is translated above as "have sex," does not always refer to knowing in a sexual way. It may mean to get to know someone in a purely social way.

That's true. But words don't receive meanings in a vacuum. Context determines meaning. The word *trunk* can refer to an elephant's nose or the rear luggage compartment of a car, depending on the context. So what is the context of *yada* in Genesis 19? The sin of homosexuality. Would men try to knock down a door to extend a social visit to some strangers? Obviously not. The aggressive behavior of the men of Sodom was a product of their homosexual desires, not a casual desire to meet some new friends. In fact, the second option doesn't even make sense in light of God's judgment on Sodom and its neighbor, Gomorrah. Would God have destroyed their inhabitants for merely being self-centered and socially aggressive? Noted educator and theologian Dr. Kenneth Gangel gives the most reasonable answer: "To be sure, there were other sins in Sodom as there have been in every city of every nation throughout all the times of man. But we know of only one episode in history where God singled out a particular sin and destroyed two entire cities because of it—the sin was homosexuality and the cities were Sodom and Gomorrah."[6]

People of the Same Gender Should Not Have Sex

In a public forum, a practicing homosexual and professing Christian told several reporters that the Bible does not condemn homosexuality. I quoted to him Leviticus 18:22 which states, "Do not lie with a man as one lies with a woman; that is detestable." Although I caught him off guard, he regained his composure and said, "But it also says that it's wrong to have sex during a woman's period." He avoided my question because he could not answer it. So I pointed out that limitations on normal intercourse for hygienic purposes is a lot different from saying sex between two men is "detestable." To that he had nothing to say.

Today's advocates of homosexuality discount this teaching in the Levitical code as purely cultural. But they fail to understand the difference between ceremonial laws and moral laws. Ceremonial laws, such as dietary practices and ritualistic cleansing, were temporary and time-bound as part of a now-obsolete covenant (Heb. 8:13). Moral laws, on the other hand, are unchanging and timeless, reflecting the character of God. That's why nine of the ten commandments are repeated in the New Testament. And that's why homosexuality is condemned, not only in the Old Testament, but also in Romans 1:24–27 and Jude 7.

While the moral law governing homosexuality has not changed, the punishment for it has. Under Old Testament law those who practiced homosexual sex could receive the death penalty: "If a man lies with a man as one lies with a woman, both of them have done what is detestable. They must be put to death; their blood will be on their own heads" (Lev. 20:13). Why no death penalty in our day? Because God's mercy has been extended to all of us, including the homosexual offender. God has postponed judgment to allow all of us to repent.

Homosexuality and Lesbianism Are Unnatural

Under the control of the Holy Spirit, the apostle Paul wrote about people who rejected the message of salvation.

> For although they knew God, they neither glorified him as God nor gave thanks to him, but their thinking became futile and their foolish hearts were darkened. Although they claimed to be wise, they became fools and exchanged the glory of the immortal God for images made to look like mortal man and birds and animals and reptiles.
>
> Therefore God gave them over in the sinful desires of their hearts to sexual impurity for the degrading of their bodies with one another. They exchanged the truth of God for a lie, and worshiped and served created things rather than the Creator—who is forever praised. Amen.
>
> Because of this, God gave them over to shameful lusts. Even their women exchanged natural relations for unnatural ones. In the same way the men also abandoned natural relations with women and were inflamed with lust for one another. Men committed indecent acts with other men, and received in themselves the due penalty for their perversion.
>
> Furthermore, since they did not think it worthwhile to retain the

knowledge of God, he gave them over to a depraved mind, to do what ought not to be done (Rom. 1:21–28).

Note the downward progression. These people knew about God from creation but failed to glorify Him. An ungrateful heart led to futile thinking, which in turn created an even more foolish, darkened heart. So they turned to worshiping the creation rather than the Creator. Then the Creator allowed them to fall prey to their own sins as they surrendered themselves to sexual immorality and degrading passions—including unnatural desires for someone of the same sex.

What homosexual advocates say about this passage verges on the ludicrous. They suggest that *unnatural* refers to bisexuals who have abandoned their previous sexual orientation. In other words, if you were born a homosexual and remain a homosexual, you are living within natural boundaries. But the context clearly teaches that what's natural is the union of a man and a woman as designed by God. Sexual union between members of the same sex is unnatural—a tragic, sinful deviation from God's design.

Homosexuals Can Be Forgiven

Evangelical responses to homosexuality range from complete acceptance to hostile rejection. Some Christians seek to love the homosexual by endorsing the lifestyle. Others reject the lifestyle so adamantly that they seem to hate the homosexual. Ideally, we should love the person and hate the sin. Of course, that's easier to say than to do. But it becomes easier when we realize that homosexuality is not an unforgivable sin. As Paul said centuries ago:

Do you not know that the wicked will not inherit the kingdom of God? Do not be deceived: Neither the sexually immoral nor idolaters nor adulterers nor male prostitutes nor homosexual offenders nor thieves nor the greedy nor drunkards nor slanderers nor swindlers will inherit the kingdom of God. And that is what some of you were. But you were washed, you were sanctified, you were justified in the name of the Lord Jesus Christ and by the Spirit of our God (1 Cor. 6:9–11).

"And that is what some of you *were*." Past tense. Homosexuals can be forgiven. Not only that, they can stop being practicing homosexuals. Some believers in Corinth had been homosexuals. But through Christ, they found forgiveness, cleansing, and restoration.

Several important lessons surface in this passage:

1. Homosexuality must not be acceptable if abandoning the life is commended.
2. Homosexuality is a matter of choice; otherwise change would not be possible.
3. Homosexuals can be saved and delivered from their sin.
4. When individuals continue in a pattern of sexual sin, it may well indicate they never became Christians. I am not saying they may lose their salvation. What I am saying is that outward actions reveal inner realities.

The Bible clearly condemns homosexuality. From a scriptural perspective, it cannot be considered an "alternate lifestyle." But the Bible does offer both eternal and temporal hope to the person caught in the homosexual maze.

What Homosexuality Is Not

While searching for identity in the early teen years, a child can become the victim of a homosexual overture. A man I counseled was introduced to homosexuality at the age of seventeen by a clergyman. Since then he has classified himself as a homosexual. If he had been prepared to reject this initial encounter, the course of his life could have been different. To help our children walk on the fulfilling path of heterosexual monogamy, we must explode the myths being cultivated by the homosexual community.

The first myth is that homosexuality is caused by biological, hormonal, or genetic factors. With modern technology, we could easily identify a specific trait that predisposes one toward such a lifestyle. Instead, hundreds of clinical studies have failed to find any such connection. We can only conclude that men and women adopt a homosexual or lesbian lifestyle based on previous experience and exposure.

Another myth is that one is a homosexual merely because of an affection for a member of the same sex. But in the Old Testament

Jonathan and David shared a profound love, which honored, not defamed, God. When they departed company following an angry outburst by King Saul, they kissed each other and wept. But this was a perfectly appropriate Semitic expression of their deep friendship, not of a sexual relationship. Semitic people have always been very expressive. That by no means indicates a homosexual relationship. The fact is, feelings and emotions do not determine sexual orientation. Our children can feel a natural, wholesome closeness to a friend of the same sex without that leading to or indicating a homosexual lifestyle.

In view of what is taking place in our society, love must be clearly defined apart from sexual expression. We can love someone without needing any sexual expression of that love. Once a child understands the difference between affection and sexual orientation, we can carefully discuss the temptation to engage in a homosexual act. While many young people will not even think about homosexual sex, others will be tempted.

Let me model for you the way I would communicate some of these concepts. Assume a conversation with a teenage boy:

> *Son, you are at an exciting but difficult time in your life. It's exciting because God wants to use you to help change this world. But it's also a difficult time because you are not old enough to be married and yet you have strong sexual desires.*
>
> *There are people, homosexuals, who will tell you that you can express those desires with other boys or men. As you know, that's not how God made us. Don't ever assume that just because you care about one of your friends that you are a homosexual. Men can love other men without sex having anything to do with their relationship. Don't let anyone confuse you.*
>
> *Remember, you can talk to me about anything—including this. I love you, and I always will.*

By communicating this way, you can accomplish three things:

- You will demonstrate your open acceptance of your child's sexuality;

- You will help your child understand that in certain situations he may become confused about his sexual orientation;
- You will encourage him to come to talk to you if he finds himself confused.

There can be nothing more open and honest than such a conversation. Children need to have an open door to speak to us even about an issue that they know would cause us great concern. Some parents actually push their children into the arms of homosexuals by failing to initiate such unconditional love and acceptance.

What happened to Jerry Arterburn need not happen to your child. When Jerry was five, he was molested by an older boy at a church camp—the same night he accepted Jesus Christ as his Savior. He didn't feel he could talk to his mom so he lived with his secret even as his sexuality took a tail spin into the confusing world of homosexuality. It wasn't until Jerry was dying of AIDS that he finally opened up and admitted to his mother that he was living in a way he knew was wrong. When communication began to flow, he finally experienced the love and acceptance of his family—a love and acceptance he could have known many years before.

Our children need to know that we will accept them completely, no matter what their struggles might be. This will encourage them to allow us to guide them through their stormy teen years so that they will land on the shore of heterosexual, monogamous sexual fulfillment.

GIVE IT SOME THOUGHT

1. Is your child fully aware of the danger of molestation? Does he or she have the foresight to anticipate threatening situations?

2. What are some day-to-day circumstances that might compel you to talk about homosexuality?

3. What does your child know about homosexuality? Can you guess the source of the information?

4. Does your son understand that a spontaneous erection in the company of other boys or men does not mean he is a homosexual?

5. Does your child understand that affection for a member of the same sex does not mean he or she is a homosexual?

6. Will your child come to you when he or she experiences a sexual identity crisis?

CHAPTER 13

AIDS and STDs

She had learned a difficult lesson the hard way. It took months, but she had regained her dignity and self-respect. There were fewer tears. In their place was a growing commitment to Jesus Christ. Her former lover, the rebel son of the local pastor, had become merely a memory. God had forgiven her. Now she wanted to sin no more. Despite the joy of her new life and renewed faith, when the boyfriend who had jilted her showed up at her door, she was flooded with guilt and paralyzed with pain.

"What do you want?" she asked with a trembling voice.

"I need to talk with you."

She held back the tears. "We don't have anything to talk about."

She expected the usual temper tantrum that never came. Instead, he stared at the ground. After what seemed like an eternity, he began to choke out his reason for coming. "I decided to join the Marines and they gave me a test . . . a blood test. They said I have AIDS. They told me to tell you so you could have the test done." Then he just turned and walked away.

She stood there, feeling violated once again and fearing for her life. With tears streaming down her cheeks and her body shaking uncontrollably, she closed the door and turned to face her dad, who was sitting close by. Could she hide it from him? She wanted to in the worst way. But her past had placed her future in jeopardy. She needed his help. For a fleeting moment she considered what it would be like to take the test without Mom and Dad knowing. But she knew she couldn't go it alone.

"Dad, I need to take a test . . . for—AIDS."

AIDS—A MATTER OF LIFE AND DEATH

Children, young people, teenagers are dying from AIDS. More will. Christian children, whose sexual conduct varies little from their unbelieving counterparts, are by no means immune.

How concerned should parents be? As concerned as Surgeon General C. Everett Koop who said, "I am petrified. . . . The number of cases is doubling every thirteen months, and youngsters are the most vulnerable."[1] Why are they so vulnerable? Because they are sexually active and feel they are invincible.

If someone has sex just one time with the wrong person, he or she can get AIDS. AIDS is fatal. There is no known cure or vaccination. Dr. Koop doubts we will ever find a cure and does not expect a vaccination before the year 2000. Sex has become a matter of life and death.

Just one sexual encounter is enough for a person to contract the fatal virus. As the number of carriers increases, the chance of exposure does as well. Research scientist Mathilde Krim has stated, "In a large metropolitan area, . . . the risk of any young person meeting a new sexual partner who is already infected is between one in 10 and one in 20. That is a very substantial risk, because there is no going back."[2]

WHY AIDS IS DIFFICULT TO DISCUSS

It is tough enough talking to our children about sex. Now we have to give them the facts about AIDS. That seems to demand that we discuss explicit homosexual behavior. Who feels comfortable talking about anal intercourse? Deviancy will always be difficult to explain, because by its very nature it is irrational.

AIDS is also tough to discuss because young people think they are impregnable. They refuse to accept the possibility that they could get a fatal disease. Studies suggest that sexually active young people who have a thorough knowledge of AIDS still do not really believe they are at risk. They know the facts, but they don't see the application to their own lives.

Another difficulty in discussing AIDS is the paradox of purity and protection. Should we tell our children that if they can't be pure, they ought at least to be protected? Do we dare say "Wait" in one breath, then add "But if you can't, wear a condom"?

Confusing and at times contradictory evidence also makes AIDS education very difficult. An executive administrator of a large hospital, having met with officials of the United States Department of Health and Human Services, told me, "When AIDS first surfaced they said there was nothing to worry about. Now they are saying that a staggering percentage of the population could get infected. I don't know who to believe." If you have followed the various medical reports, you have discovered that medical researchers do not agree on the future danger or transmittability of the disease. For example, the Surgeon General's Report on AIDS states: "There is no known risk of non-sexual infection in most of the situations we encounter in our daily lives. We know that family members living with individuals who have the AIDS virus do not become infected except through sexual contact. There is no evidence of transmission (spread) of the AIDS virus by everyday contact even though these family members shared food, towels, cups, razors, even toothbrushes, and kissed each other."[3]

But in contrast to the Surgeon General's Report, a memorandum by Dr. John Seale of the Royal Society of Medicine states: "Moderately efficient means of transmission include mouth-to-mouth and genital contact before and during normal sexual intercourse, oral salivary contact between small children, needle-stick injuries to nursing staff, and chance contact of sores or abrasions with blood, serum, saliva or sputum."[4]

The issues are complicated, the information, confusing, and our response, critical. But, no matter how difficult issues are, parents are still best suited to teach their children about the death threat of AIDS. Indeed, we *must* educate our kids about it.

WHAT IS AIDS?

The letters A-I-D-S stand for acquired immune deficiency syndrome. AIDS is caused by a virus. The virus itself is designated as HIV, or human immunodeficiency virus. A person can have the virus without any apparent symptoms. Although he may feel fine, he can transmit the disease to others.

The AIDS virus invades the genetic code of immune cells. When the immune cells begin to reproduce themselves, the AIDS virus reproduces itself and eventually destroys the body's immune system. As immune cells are depleted, the body loses the capacity to fight off even minor diseases. When the body's defensive capacity has been destroyed the person falls victim to acute illnesses and experiences nausea, sore throat, and swollen glands.

In the early stage of the disease, the patient is said to have ARC or AIDS-related complex. In the more advanced stages, AIDS-related illnesses become chronic, with respiratory infections being the most common. While diseases take advantage of the disabled immune system, the AIDS virus may also attack the brain, causing disorientation and dementia.

HOW DOES A PERSON GET AIDS?

Medical evidence indicates AIDS spreads primarily through body fluids such as blood, semen, and vaginal secretions. It has also been found in urine, sweat, tears, and saliva. Many researchers discount the possibility of getting AIDS from urine, sweat, tears, and saliva because these typically have a low concentration of the virus. But there are credible individuals who maintain that body fluids such as saliva and sweat may be able to transmit the virus. So it appears that time and additional research are needed to absolutely prove the premise that AIDS cannot be transmitted through more casual contact. Dr. John Seale, in his Report to the House of Commons in London, states that other forms of transmission may be possible though inefficient:

Inefficient means of transmission include social kissing, inhalation or respiratory aerosols caused by coughing or sneezing, and blood-sucking insects.

Transmission by inhalation is only inefficient because of the relatively small number of virions shed in saliva and bronchial secretions. However, if an AIDS virion is inhaled into the lung it is engulfed by an amoeba-like macrophage on the lining of the alveoli (air sacs). It has been shown repeatedly in the laboratory that the AIDS virus readily infects macrophages, and the virus replicates within them, thereby enabling infection of people to be initiated by this route.[5]

While we do not want to be paralyzed by panic, we can only conclude that when professionals disagree on how a life-threatening virus is transmitted, the best thing we could do is err in favor of protection. Common sense dictates that until we have time-tested, undeniable evidence to the contrary, we must take precautions against getting AIDS even from saliva.

In a discussion with a very knowledgeable, conservative internist, I asked if kissing could place our children at risk. He felt the risk was minimal but suggested that the risk was far greater when eating in restaurants where AIDS carriers handle food.

Therefore, until incontrovertible evidence is amassed concerning the transmission of AIDS, each of us will need to decide what precautions to take to avoid exposure in light of the information we have. As more definitive information becomes available, we may be able to eliminate some present concerns.

THE HOLOCAUST AHEAD

Health and Human Services Secretary Otis Bowen, comparing typhus, small pox, and the black plague to the AIDS epidemic, said these will "look very pale by comparison . . . You haven't read or heard of anything yet."[6]

The Center for Disease Control (CDC) has estimated that the number of actual cases of AIDS in the United States will grow from 27 thousand in 1986 to 270 thousand in 1991. Worldwide cases of AIDS will increase from 36 thousand to as high as 3 million in the same time frame. The CDC also estimates that the number of infected people in the United States will grow from 1 to 2 million in 1986 to 3 to 5 million in 1991. Global estimates range from 5 to 10 million in 1986 to between 50 and 100 million in 1991.[7] If CDC's estimates are correct, almost as many people will die of AIDS in 1991 as died in the entire Vietnam War. The death count in 1991 could exceed 54 thousand people with health care costs of at least $32 billion.[8]

WHAT THE SCRIPTURES SAY
ABOUT AIDS AND STDs

Sexually transmitted diseases (STDs) have been with us for a long time, dating back as far as ancient Israel. Proverbs 5 presents a father's warning to his son that he not be enticed by the sensuous speech of an adulteress. After pointing out how she operates, he exhorts his son to stay away from her door lest he pay an incredible price for an unholy union. Then he graphically describes the potential consequences: "At the end of your life you will groan, / when your flesh and body are spent" (v. 11). What an apt description of someone dying of STDs or even AIDS.

This proverb draws a direct connection between sexual sin and life-threatening disease and death. As one commentator notes:

> Verse 11 is explicit about one effect of adultery; illicit sexual activity brings on venereal disease which often proves excruciatingly fatal.
>
> Eventually the man who succumbs to lust is reduced to poverty, disgrace, and disease. It is too late, however, for regrets. He can only utter a long litany of "if onlys": if only I had listened to my father; if only I hadn't gone my own way; if only I had taken others' advice; if only I could have known an hour of pleasure would result in a lifetime of regret.[9]

In ancient Israel, people died from sexually transmitted diseases. Without antibiotics, many STDs would prove fatal in our day. Now we have AIDS, which is often transmitted sexually, depletes the body's resources, and cannot be fought with antibiotics. At the end of their lives, AIDS victims groan as their flesh and body are spent.

Psalm 38, from the pen of King David, also describes diseases as the natural consequence of sin. We cannot be certain, but the sickness David describes could have been a sexually transmitted disease.

> Because of your wrath there is no health in my body;
> my bones have no soundness because of my sin.
> My guilt has overwhelmed me
> like a burden too heavy to bear.
> My wounds fester and are loathsome
> because of my sinful folly.
> I am bowed down and brought very low;
> all day long I go about mourning.
> My back is filled with searing pain;

there is no health in my body.
I am feeble and utterly crushed;
I groan in anguish of heart.   (Ps. 38:3–8)

When you read the words of the psalmist, can't you just see the bedridden AIDS patient whose body is pierced with pain?

In teaching your child about AIDS and other STDs, read this passage and then focus on verse 5, which establishes a cause-and-effect relationship between "sinful folly" and festering, loathsome sores.

Another passage you will want to share with your child is found in Paul's letter to the believers at Rome: "Because of this, God gave them over to shameful lusts. . . . Men committed indecent acts with other men, and received in themselves the due penalty for their perversion" (Rom. 1:26–27).

This passage condemns homosexual activity and refers to a penalty incurred by those who practice indecent, perverted acts. The penalty ranges from a depraved mind to disease. AIDS is a natural penalty for promiscuity and perversion.

Although AIDS has also become a heterosexual problem in the United States, it started in the homosexual population and spread rapidly as a result of homosexual and bisexual behavior. Many early cases of AIDS have been traced to "Patient 0," a homosexual flight attendant who had 150 to 200 different sex partners a year for ten years. Imagine, one homosexual man had over a thousand illicit sexual encounters and personally infected hundreds of people.

In the late 1970s, Patient 0's doctor told him, "I don't know what this disease is that you have, but I can only assume it will eventually kill you and that it is transmitted sexually. You have got to stop exposing others." Patient 0 replied, "It's my body, and I'll do what I want to with it."

Discussing AIDS and other sexually transmitted diseases in a biblical context will build your children's confidence in God's Word as they understand He is not surprised by what is happening. Once you have explained the facts about AIDS and read through the relevant passages with your child, summarize this way:

If you have sex just one time with a person who has AIDS, you can get the disease and you will die from it. But if you follow God's

perfect plan for sexual fulfillment—you and your wife (husband) will
enjoy sex without any fear of disease. Keep in mind, if you get AIDS,
every time you have sex you may give the disease to the other person
who will die from it. Make sure to do what God says. Don't sin
sexually. You may later discover you have AIDS.

These exhortations to protective purity must be straightforward
and regularly repeated. The messages of mortality and morality
must convince our youth of the dangers of AIDS.

GOALS FOR DISCUSSING AIDS AND STDs

What do we want to accomplish when we talk to our children
about AIDS? Let me suggest two goals. First, we must demonstrate
that purity offers protection. It's not enough simply to tell a young
person of the dangers of AIDS. As Surgeon General Koop has said,
"Young people today—who think they're immortal . . . have to be
taught to ask, 'Is this experience worth dying for?' Abstinence is
the only way you can be perfectly protected. The next is through the
establishment of a mutually faithful monogamous relationship."[10]

The second goal is to teach spiritual truths so our children develop a biblical perspective on AIDS and STDs. This goal has several dimensions we need to explore.

The Spiritual Dimension

Why does AIDS exist? Where did it come from? Why can't we
find a cure? Why do so many innocent people die from it? These are
some of the questions we all have in response to the AIDS epidemic. But many people in our society usually want only scientific
answers, not ethical ones. A doctor who has extensively studied the
epidemiology of AIDS made a statement that I fear reflects the attitude many other professionals have toward the disease. He told me
as far as he was concerned, it was merely a virus and ethical questions were not his concern.

But it's far more than a virus. It's a disease that flourishes because of sexual sin and perversion. We cannot adequately understand or fight the disease until we deal with the behavior that caused
it. If we don't counter the behavior, we can look forward to more
suffering and death, some of which may be caused by still more
lethal sexual diseases. So we must counter the spread of disease by

looking to God's Word and teaching it to our kids, from infancy onward.

SPIRITUAL LESSONS FOR YOUNG CHILDREN

AIDS puts parents in a very awkward position. If we do not tell our children enough, we could jeopardize their health and well-being. On the other hand, telling a young child about homosexuality seems downright abusive. I think the solution lies in telling our children enough to protect them, but not telling them so much as to frighten or confuse them. When children know they should not allow anyone to touch their genitals, explaining sexual perversion should not be necessary.

Several spiritual lessons can be engraved on the minds of younger children who will grow up in the age of AIDS.

If we obey God's Word and live the way God wants us to live, we will have little chance of ever getting AIDS. In talking about AIDS, make a strong association between health and obedience. Then when your child asks, "What is AIDS?" you might respond this way:

> *AIDS is a disease. Right now everyone who gets AIDS dies from it. Most people get AIDS because they don't use their bodies the way God intended. They didn't listen and obey God, so they got this terrible disease.*

Let me warn you that some children will want more specific information or clarification. It won't always demand a heavy response. Their questions may even be humorous. One mother said the above to her eight-year-old daughter, who took the palm of her hand and pushed her nose flat to her face and said, "You mean Pee Wee Herman will get AIDS because he pushes his nose up like this?" So be prepared! Anything may come up.

God wants us to protect our bodies from disease by keeping them clean, eating the right foods, and exercising. Proper hygiene will protect our children from all forms of disease, including AIDS. When they understand this, it builds into their minds a respect for their body as a gift from God.

At a conference I attended, an expert in infectious diseases told me that if we washed our hands regularly, we would dramatically reduce the incidence of infectious disease.

Hygienic and dietary practices teach volumes to our young children. Without even a word they learn, "The body is not meant for sexual immorality, but for the Lord, and the Lord (is) for the body" (1 Cor. 6:13).

There are people who hate God and refuse to do what He says. At an early age, Christian children naturally develop an "us and them" mentality, which comes from drawing contrasts between Christians and non-Christians. The intensity of the moral swing of our day will make the spiritual disparities all the more potent.

Label dangerous behaviors, such as nonmarital sex and drug use, as non-Christian in nature. Without denying that believers might engage in these behaviors, simply stress that if a person strives to live as a Christian, he or she will not do certain things. With my children I often ask, "Is that what a Christian would do? Is that the way a Christian would behave?" This challenges a child to view actions as either acceptable or unacceptable to God.

SPIRITUAL LESSONS FOR ADOLESCENTS AND TEENS

Several profound lessons can be sown in the minds of our older youth. In the fertile soil of concern over AIDS, let's plant spiritual truth.

God will not be mocked. We will reap what we sow. As Paul's letter to the Galatians states: "God cannot be mocked. A man reaps what he sows. The one who sows to please his sinful nature, from that nature will reap destruction; the one who sows to please the Spirit will reap eternal life" (Gal. 6:7–8).

Our God will not allow people to sin and not pay a price for that sin. Homosexuality, premarital sex, and adultery are vain attempts to mock God's plan for a sexual relationship. They all lead to personal destruction and divine condemnation.

Christian youth should understand that God's forgiveness does not usually protect us from suffering the natural consequences of disobedience. Being a Christian does not protect a person from getting AIDS. Living as a Christian will. If our children sow purity, they will reap marital pleasure. If they sow sexual sin, they are likely to reap sickness, disease, and death.

There is an AIDS of the human spirit. AIDS illustrates in the physical realm what happens in the spiritual realm when we sin sexually. How many stories of AIDS deaths have you witnessed on the television newscasts and specials? I have lost count. Although the programs sometimes focus on the innocent hemophiliac who contracted the disease from a transfusion, they generally zero in on accounts of homosexual couples. The camera documents the rapid deterioration of the emaciated victim whose body is riddled with sores.

After viewing one of these tragic scenes, I realized that I was seeing in the physical arena what I had seen so many times in the spiritual realm. There is an AIDS of the human spirit. When people sin sexually and give themselves over to degradation, their emotional and spiritual suffering is as painful as the dreaded disease. They feel ashamed and cut off from God, alienated from themselves and the Lord who loves them.

AIDS is a natural penalty for perversion and promiscuity. Even people who do not hold to a biblical ethic see AIDS as a form of divine condemnation:

> Public bewilderment at the disease is taking many forms. Conservative leaders see it as a summons to chastity or monogamy. Many people, dealing with the absolute death sentence that AIDS imposes, consider it a vague sort of retribution, an Old Testament-style revenge. Says a Los Angeles entertainment writer: "Sexual disease has been around for thousands of years. It reappears when monogamy breaks down. AIDS pushes monogamy right back up there on the priority list."[11]

AIDS initially spread throughout the United States as a result of deviant homosexual practices. Should you tell your child about these deviant acts? If you don't, someone else will. You really don't have a choice, especially since homosexual practices such as anal intercourse, oral genital sex, rimming (oral-anal contact), fisting (anal/rectal penetration with a fist), water sports (drinking and spraying urine), and fecal ingestion are rapidly transmitting the virus. If their first exposure is in a health class at school or from their friends, these horrible homosexual practices may be presented as acceptable, even normal. That could lead to beliefs and practices which could devastate our children down the road.

In the chapter on homosexuality, I gave some guidelines for discussing this unacceptable lifestyle with your child. Since most AIDS victims in America are from the homosexual population, it may be necessary to address these together.

AIDS AND "SAFE SEX"

"John, when I said it, I felt like I had let the Lord down."

Those words came from a close friend after he talked to his eighteen-year-old son about AIDS and "safe sex." He described how he challenged his son to live for the Lord and to wait until marriage for a sexual relationship. His son seemed to accept the challenge. Yet mindful of the AIDS death threat, my friend stopped at the end of the conversation and said, "But if you do decide to have sex, make sure you wear a condom."

His son responded indignantly, "Dad, I am going to do what's right."

Should a parent say, "Sex outside marriage is wrong, but if you decide to do it anyway, make sure to wear a condom"? Many Christian parents I talk to are advising their children to wear a condom if they should decide to have sex before marriage. What happens when we take such an approach? For one thing, we communicate a lack of confidence in our children. Whether we mean to or not, we tell them that we cannot absolutely trust them to do what is right. In the face of this tendency, the Bible says, "Love . . . always trusts," or always expects the best, of the one being loved (1 Cor. 13:7).

When we recommend condoms we are also teaching our children that the consequences of their behavior are more serious than the behavior itself. To put it another way, it's as if we said, "If you can get away with it, it's fine." But that's like lying to protect a person from being justly punished. The lie doesn't become true or right simply because it may produce desirable consequences. The lie remains a lie. Both the actions lied about and the lying are wrong. So no matter how you slice it, promoting condom use outside of marriage implicitly endorses nonmarital sex. If we promote it, we are offering a wrong alternative when a legitimate, guaranteed alternative exists—namely, abstinence until marriage.

There's another serious problem with suggesting the use of a condom. Condoms are not guaranteed to protect a person from disease. The foil wrapper of a name-brand condom reads: "While no contraceptive provides 100% protection, Trojan brand condoms can aid in the prevention of pregnancy. Trojan brand condoms, when properly used, can also aid in reducing the risk of spreading many sexually transmitted diseases."

Imagine how you would feel if you told your teenager to wear a condom if he had sex, only to have him come to you sometime later with the news that he has had sex with a girl and fears he could have AIDS. Then he describes for you how the condom came off after they had intercourse.

In a matter of life and death, we should not take any chances. Using a condom offers some protection but certainly not absolute safety. We do need to talk with our children about condoms, but we must be very careful *not* to offer condom use as a viable alternative to abstinence. The *way* we communicate is as important as *what* we communicate. Let me suggest a way to inform your teenage son of condoms without endorsing their use.

> *Son, you can get AIDS while having sex or when using dirty needles. Semen, blood, and vaginal secretions transmit the AIDS virus. A person who decides to disobey God and have sex just once could get AIDS and eventually die from it.*
>
> *You have heard commercials and advertisements that say with condoms you can have "safe sex." But there is no guarantee that condoms will protect you from getting AIDS. Just read the sides of the condom packages. They offer some protection when properly used, but they are not guaranteed. The only way to be truly safe is to wait until marriage to have sex. Even if condoms were 100 percent effective, they would not prevent "AIDS of the human spirit"— heartaches because you have dishonored God and defrauded some young lady. The emotional and spiritual pain can be as bad as the physical pain.*

Never before in human history has there been such a tremendous motivation to follow God's plan for sexual expression. Our children can be the benefactors or the victims of the AIDS epidemic. Benefactors, if they see and accept God's wisdom in waiting until marriage to have sex. Victims, if they don't. As we direct them with God's Word and challenge them to appropriate God's power, the resulting purity will protect them in our age of perversion.

GIVE IT SOME THOUGHT

1. Does your child know the essential facts about AIDS and sexually transmitted diseases? If not, when and how do you plan to tell him or her?

2. Is your child's behavior putting him or her at risk for contracting AIDS from blood, semen, vaginal secretions, or saliva? If so, what can you do about it?

3. How does your child feel about God's role in the AIDS epidemic? Does your child think God is wrong for allowing it to happen? Prepare yourself to discuss this with your child.

4. How does your child feel about "safe sex"? If you don't know, how can you find out?

5. Does your child really understand and appreciate the death threat of AIDS? If you're not sure, set some time aside to educate your child.

6. What does your child's school teach about AIDS and "safe sex"? If you're unsure, find out so that you can either reinforce or counteract what is being taught.

7. Does your child carry condoms, anticipating using them? What impact will this practice have on his or her commitment to purity?

APPENDIX A

Biblical Answers to Some Tough Questions

Q: When should my teenager be allowed to date?

A: Few questions stir the hearts and minds of parents and children alike as this one. Since my daughter was a little girl I have openly stated she should be allowed to date at the tender age of twenty-seven!

To answer this question I would like to pose another more revealing question. Namely, at what age can your teenager handle the sexual temptation which tends to be a part of the dating scene? Sexual temptation is the key issue and we should address it directly when it comes to dating. Don't avoid the obvious when discussing dating with your teen.

Ideally, dating should take place in an environment that encourages healthy social interaction between young men and young women while minimizing sexual temptation. Young people need to learn to relate to each other as persons and not just as physical objects.

Several biblical truths offer direct counsel on the question of dating:

1. We are to flee from sexual immorality, not fight it! (1 Corinthians 6:18) The best example of this may be Joseph's response to Potiphar's wife as recorded in Genesis 39:12. If Joseph had stayed around to discuss her sexual solicitation, he would have been a "goner."
2. We flee temptation, mindful of the strong sexual desires of youth. "Flee the evil desires of youth, and pursue righteous-

ness, faith, love and peace, along with those who call on the Lord out of a pure heart"(2 Tim. 2:22). Keep in mind Paul's commands were written to Timothy, who was a young pastor. He told him to flee the evil desires which are present, especially in young people. Because Timothy was unmarried, the sexual gratification of these desires would be an offense against God. In this passage Paul gives a three-fold admonition to Timothy and our young people. Consider his words in light of dating:

Flee temptation.

Focus on what is good.

Fellowship with others who pursue purity.

Communicating these concepts will not be easy, but let me suggest how you might get started. In this case you are talking with your daughter.

Sweetheart, I know you want to date, and I too want you to get to know other young people, including young men. Here are my concerns. Dating easily becomes a situation where you and/or your date will be tempted sexually. I know you want to live for the Lord so we must keep in mind what God says (read and explain 1 Cor. 6:18, 2 Tim. 2:22). In view of what God says it seems best that you avoid social situations that open the door to sexual temptation. Secondly, it is obviously important that you spend time with other young people who want to live for the Lord.

One closing thought as you work through the issue of dating: most young people have an intense desire to date because of peer pressure. Dating is a social and cultural phenomenon. In New Testament times dating did not occur and marriages were arranged.

It may be comfortable to conform, but we will have to surrender our convictions in order to do so. As our society morally decays, we will find ourselves having to fight the tendency to conform to this world (Rom. 12:2). Don't assume that dating as practiced in our day must be a given when it comes to your child's experience.

Q: My teenage daughter has started dating a young man whom I don't trust. Should I say something to her?

A: You may want to say something to her, but I would also suggest that you say something to him. I know of parents who pointedly, yet politely, interrogate their daughters' dates. I consider it both acceptable and advisable, especially with the phenomenon of date rape. One dad who took this approach would tell his daughter's date, "My daughter is a Christian and belongs to Jesus Christ who lives within her. To honor Him she has decided to remain a virgin until marriage. She will not have sex before marriage. Do you have any problem with that?" Wouldn't you just love to have a videotape of a teenage boy hearing those words?

Q: What telltale signs can a parents look for when their adolescent or teen is struggling with sexual desires?

A: When a young person reaches puberty, it's safe to assume the struggle has begun. You can make a number of observations to try to determine the intensity of your child's struggle.

Do you suspect your teen is masturbating frequently? How does your son look at girls? Have you found pornographic magazines in your teen's possession? How does your daughter talk about boys? Does she emphasize only their looks and not their personalities? When with a member of the opposite sex, does your teen constantly need to be touching?

Answering these and comparable questions should help you gauge your teen's battle with sexual desires.

Q: My teenage son says I have no right to go through his dresser drawers. I disagree. What do you think?

A: Why not go through his mind rather than through his dresser drawers? Ask him what he's doing, and spend enough time with him to see it first hand. Get close enough in the relationship so that you really do know what's going on. Tell him if he will level with you, then he can have his privacy. If he won't, tell him that you are concerned, not just curious. Then discuss some of the dangers that exist in our sexually sick society.

Q: I find it very difficult to teach my teenager about sex. One subject I can't bring myself to discuss is oral sex. Do I really need to talk about it?

A: Your sensitivity is certainly understandable, but our society gives us no choice. A great many teens are involved in oral sex. In fact, some Christian young people who view premarital intercourse as wrong consider oral genital sex as acceptable.

While oral sex may be an acceptable form of expression between a husband and wife, it certainly is unacceptable outside of marriage.

Oral sex is wrong outside the marriage relationship for several reasons:

1. God's provision for passion is marital union (1 Cor. 7:1–4).
2. Oral sex outside marriage involves lust, and lust is sin (Matt. 5:27–30).
3. The intimacy of oral sex can easily defraud the other person, robbing the person of self-respect (1 Thess. 4:3–6).

Young people must understand that sex is far more than intercourse. It involves a sacred union in which two people give themselves after having committed to a lifelong relationship.

Q: How can I tell if my child is sexually active? What signs should I be looking for?

A: Sexual activity does affect a young person's behavior. The physical act unleashes a myriad of emotions and spiritual struggles. A young person who becomes sexually active will probably demonstrate guilt symptoms which include an aversion to spiritual things and the desire to pull away from Mom and Dad. If your child won't look you in the eyes or turns her head whenever you address spiritual matters, you have to begin to suspect that something is wrong. Anything or anyone who reminds her that she is wrong will instigate a guilt response that often is seen in the form of anger.

Also, keep in mind, sexual desires, when they are fed, tend to dominate a young person's mind. If a teen manipulates a parent to get alone with a boyfriend or a girlfriend, suspect sexual involvement.

Q: I see a number of signs that my child *is* sexually involved. What should I do? We have not been close for some time.

A: Since you do not have an open and honest relationship with effective communication, anything you do probably will not work and may even make matters worse. Begin by investing time with your child in a positive atmosphere; defrost the frozen communication lines with relaxed and informal interaction. Have fun together doing something he or she enjoys. Then begin to look for gestures that indicate your child's heart is opened to you. Is there eye contact and spontaneous conversation and spiritual closeness and touching? Once these begin to surface, pray for the opportunity to ask about your child's sexual behavior.

You may discover in the course of rebuilding your relationship with your child that you have been negligent in communicating spiritual truth. Consider asking your child for forgiveness and expressing your desire to help him or her understand what God says about sex. Admit that there are a number of things you wish you had discussed years ago. But better late than never.

Q: While putting away my son's clean socks, I found a condom in his dresser. What can I do? He's only twelve.

A: Let me offer several steps to take.
1. Pray for wisdom and protection for yourself and for your son. He is terribly young to be worrying about "safe sex."
2. In a comfortable setting, when he would least expect it, ask him very directly, "Are you having sex with someone?" Observe his response to determine the truthfulness of his words. If he is uncomfortable, no matter what he says, you had better assume the worst.
3. If he is sexually involved, tell him that for his benefit you will take several steps to make sure that he stops. Have several steps in mind when you confront him:

   - You may have to inform the girl's parents.
   - You will probably have to restrict his social activity.
   - You may have to consider a better school environment.
   - It might be advisable to get your youth pastor involved.
   - Make sure to increase the time you spend together in order to build up the relationship.
   - Begin to teach him what God says about sex.

4. If he is not sexually active, ask him why he needs a condom. What does he have in mind anyway? Then proceed to discuss

with him the fact that there is no "safe sex" and that there are incredible spiritual and physical dangers in premature intimacy.

Q: My young son exhibits some effeminate behavior and I am getting more and more concerned as he gets older. What should I do?

A: God designed men and women to function and act differently. He expects parents to cultivate a boy's maleness and a girl's femaleness. If by effeminate behavior you are referring to casual gestures and mannerisms, you can probably correct the behavior by constantly praising him for appropriate male gestures. Accentuate his maleness, and if possible, ignore feminine mannerisms. If this doesn't work in a couple of months, you might want to seek professional counsel. The effeminate behavior you referred to may be far more serious. If your son only wants to play with girls, wear girls' clothes, and says he wishes he was a girl, then seek professional counsel immediately. I would also recommend that you read Dr. George Alan Reker's book, *Shaping Your Child's Sexual Identity* (Grand Rapids, MI: Baker Book House, 1982) to determine a course of action.

Q: If we overprotect our children, won't they be overwhelmed when they finally go out into the world? I have heard of some children from Christian homes who go absolutely wild.

A: Yes—if we protect our children from the negative moral influences of our world and fail to prepare them to enter this world, they may well go morally crazy.

Yes—if we protect our children and they grow up in a hostile home where they never have fun, some will go berserk when they leave.

Remember, the strategy we have presented is twofold: protection and preparation. Preparation includes explaining and exposing children to the world *under our direction*. Like the father in Proverbs 5, we describe the allurements of the world and the consequences of being trapped by them.

Granted, some young people will give themselves over to the

world no matter what we do. It's their choice, and in some cases how they were raised won't matter.

Q: What should I say to my daughter about bathing suits? What is modest?

A: Modesty has been abandoned in our day. Finding an attractive and relatively modest suit won't be easy.

There are several important concepts to communicate to your daughter about a standard of modesty.
1. Don't dishonor your body by flagrant exposure and inappropriate display. Make sure to read 1 Timothy 2:9–10, which says "I also want women to dress modestly, with decency and propriety, not with braided hair or gold or pearls or expensive clothes, but with good deeds, appropriate for women who profess to worship God."
2. Pursue inner beauty over outward adornment (1 Pet. 3:3–4).
3. Don't wrong others by tempting them with your actions or dress (1 Thess. 4:6).

A great way to impress these principles on your daughter is to point out girls who are obviously selling their sexuality. Your daughter should be able to sense that a girl who flaunts herself also cheapens herself.

Q: My five-year-old walked in on us while we were having intercourse. She walked out right away, but I know she saw us. Should I talk to her?

A: Absolutely and right away. Young children who see their parents having sex usually think that Dad is hurting Mom. Reassure her that you were sharing your bodies as God made them and it is a special way to express how much you care about each other. I know you don't want to say anything, but you really must for your child's security and comfort.

Q: My husband and I didn't become Christians until our children were entering their teens. How can we begin to undo mistakes we made in the past?

A: If your children see Jesus Christ revolutionize your lives, it will be a catalyst to change their lives no matter what they have previously learned. Let them see supernatural change in you, your marriage, and the way you relate to them.

Then, explain to your children you would love to go back and raise them according to your newfound faith, but you can't. So the best thing you can do is start now and teach them about Jesus Christ and God's Word.

Don't apologize or continue to express your regrets over the past. Just let your enthusiasm make up for lost time.

Q: My husband is not a Christian and refuses to talk to our children about sex. In fact, his attitude toward sex is so lousy I'm afraid of what he might tell them. Should I tell them instead?

A: Why not use some of the ideas in this book to talk to your husband about sex? It may be a great way to get his attention and might show him the practicality and relevancy of the Bible. Read him the Song of Solomon and explain that it's an account of marital love. Some of the more explicit portions of the Song of Solomon may motivate him to read the entire Bible. While attempting to cultivate your husband's understanding, take the initiative to talk with your children. Try not to discredit Dad. Make sure that if your children sense a disagreement, they see that it is between Dad and God, not Dad and Mom.

Q: The Bible forbids fornication, but it doesn't seem to forbid any sexual relations up to a point (necking, petting, etc.). What is the biblical basis for saying no to *all* sexual activity before marriage?

A: Let me simply list several biblical principles and directives:
1. We are to flee—not fight—the "evil desires of youth" (2 Tim. 2:22).
2. We are to "flee from sexual immorality. . ." (1 Cor. 6:18).
3. Lust is sin (Matt. 5:28).
4. Necking and petting are not "holy and honorable" ways to control your own body (1 Thess. 4:4).

5. Necking and petting may "wrong" or "take advantage" of the other person (1 Thess. 4:6).

There are practical benefits to obeying these scriptural admonitions. If you refrain from arousing yourself by necking and petting, you will be a lot less frustrated and will consequently find it easier to control your sexual desires. Why pour gasoline on a fire that you don't want to burn out of control?

To control your sexual desires is to turn away from visual, tactile and auditory sexual stimulation. Otherwise, you tempt yourself and the other person.

Q: Shouldn't the church be involved in helping our young people to deal with the tremendous pressures of our day?

A: Absolutely. In fact, our churches need to be helping parents and children alike. As the writer of Hebrews tells us: "And let us consider how we may spur one another on toward love and good deeds. Let us not give up meeting together, as some are in the habit of doing, but let us encourage one another—and all the more as you see the Day approaching" (10:24–25). Today's social upheavals may well indicate that we will soon see the day of Christ's return. Meanwhile, since we are buffeted on all sides by secular beliefs, we need to place greater emphasis on the church as a community in which we can receive encouragement and support.

The church can do a number of things to help families. For example:

1. The church can make prayer a top priority. We should gather to pray for wisdom on how to respond to the growing attacks against our faith. We should ask the Lord to erect a hedge of moral protection around our children.

2. The church can encourage accurate, relevant, practical preaching that addresses the needs of parents and children alike. No one should ever be bored by the Bible.

3. The church can have Sunday school classes that will encourage transparency while using the Scriptures to address family issues and concerns. Where else can parents find a place that allows them to admit their struggles in raising their children?

4. The church can hold special symposiums that focus on is-

sues relevant to the family. The church can and ought to be the place where parents find assistance in teaching their children about sex.

5. The church can provide family counseling. Problems never occur in isolation. People who need counseling have often developed destructive patterns in family relationships. Therefore, they will not experience long term emotional and spiritual healing without the involvement of other family members in their counseling program. Churches can usually facilitate this process by training lay counselors and drawing on the expertise of local professional Christian counselors.

6. The church can create an environment of positive peer pressure. The church youth group must be the one place where our children can go and not feel pressured to have premarital sex. If there is any pressure of any kind, it should be for purity, not immorality.

7. The church can provide healthier alternatives to many secular social events. Our young people don't have to feel like social lepers just because we refuse to allow them to attend certain movies or social functions. The church is an ideal place to provide exciting, enjoyable alternatives to typical dating opportunities that all too often invite anything from French kissing to coitus.

8. The church can give young people a place to minister. Christian service can safeguard our children from seductive allurements. When they begin to experience the joys of being used by God, their lives change and their energies refocus.

9. The church can make helpful books available. A well-stocked church library is an absolute must. Many parents are not aware of the numerous books that can help them in their efforts. Churches can remedy this problem usually with little investment.

10. The church can use its biblical obligation to discipline those engaged in sexual sin. If the church is going to call its youth to personal purity, it must first call its adults to personal purity. If we ignore sexual sin in our midst, we will reap sexual sin in the lives of our young people.

APPENDIX B

Your Child's Growing Understanding

The following chart will help you decide what you should tell your child about sex at various stages of your child's development. Of course, children mature and acquire a need to know at different ages depending on any number of factors. Nevertheless, this chart will offer general guidance in carrying out your responsibility to teach your child a biblical view of sex.

BIBLICAL CONCEPTS	APPROXIMATE AGES			
	0–5	6–10	11–14	15–18
CONCEPTION/ BIRTH	Before you were born, God had you grow in your mother's womb.	God used sperm from Dad and an egg from Mom to form you.	Out of millions of sperm from Dad and thousands of eggs from Mom, God used just one from each to form you.	Even before you were conceived, God knew you and numbered your days.
HETERO- SEXUALITY	God made a man and a woman and told them to have children.	God made a man's body so it could be joined with a woman's body to produce children.	There are people who defy God's design and have intimate physical contact with someone of the same sex.	God's design of heterosexual monogamy offers the greatest opportunity for sexual fulfillment and satisfaction.

APPROXIMATE AGES

BIBLICAL CONCEPTS	0–5	6–10	11–14	15–18
UNCONDITIONAL LOVE	The way God loves us is the way we are to love one another.	God expects us to love other people, even when we don't feel like it.	Love is much more than being physically attracted to another person. Love is doing what is best for the other person, even when we don't want to.	Love is not lust. If you really love another person, you will never do anything that could hurt that person or pull him or her away from God.
SEXUAL DESIRE			God placed sexual desires within each of us. The desires are not wrong, but how we satisfy them can be.	Your sexual desires are very strong, but with the help of the Holy Spirit, you can wait until you are married to have sex.
TEMPTATION			As your sexual desires grow, you will be tempted to have sex before you are married. God understands that and wants you to avoid situations where you will be tempted.	Recognizing and fleeing sexual temptation is critical for personal purity. Don't ask, How far can I go? Ask, How far can I flee?
HOLY SPIRIT	The Holy Spirit is God and He lives within you when you become a Christian.	The Holy Spirit lives within you and wants to tell you what to do.	The Holy Spirit wants to help you use and control your body the right way.	If you decide to sin sexually, remember, you take God, the Holy Spirit, with you.

BIBLICAL CONCEPTS	0–5	6–10	11–14	15–18
MASTURBATION		God made you so that touching your genitals will feel good.	Masturbation is a personal decision to be made only after studying the Bible and weighing practical considerations.	Masturbation can lead to obsessive, even dangerous, behavior such as autoerotic asphyxia.
SEXUAL DEVIATIONS	There are people who might try to hurt you or will try to touch your private parts.	There are people who disobey God and do not use their bodies the way God intended.	God condemns homosexuality and lesbianism as unnatural and sinful.	In addition to homosexuality and lesbianism, there are other forms of sexual perversion such as bestiality (sex with animals), pederasty (sex with children), and incest (sex with a family member).
AIDS/STDs	God wants us to take care of our bodies.	Some people get diseases and even die when they don't use their bodies the way God says they should.	If you have sex even one time with a person who has AIDS, you could get the disease and die from it.	Homosexual sex or sex outside of marriage greatly increases your chances of getting AIDS or other sexually transmitted diseases.

APPENDIX C

Key Passages—Important Lessons

Below are several important lessons on sex that come from some key scriptural passages. These lessons have been laid out as follows so you can use your Bible to teach them to your child.

GENESIS 1:27–28; 2:18–25

God created two distinct sexes (1:27).

God commanded the man and woman to have children (1:28).

The man was created incomplete and in need of a helper (2:18).

No other creature could meet the man's need (2:19–20).

God made a woman to meet the man's need (2:22–23).

The man and the woman were to join their lives and their bodies for life (2:24).

The sexual relationship was commanded before sin entered human experience (2:24–25).

2 SAMUEL 13:1–20

Feeding sexual desires creates frustration (v. 2).

Wrong friends encourage wrong behavior (vv. 3–5).

Sexual sin often involves deception (vv. 3–5).

Avoid potentially compromising situations (vv. 10–11).

Intense sexual desires can cause irrational actions (vv. 12–14).

When lust is fulfilled and desires diminish, the ensuing guilt may result in hatred (v. 15).

Once the immoral act has occurred, the damage has been done (v. 16).

Alienation, hatred, and even violence can result from sexual sin (vv. 15–16; 28–29).

PROVERBS 5

Children should be encouraged to follow their parents' wisdom (v. 1).

Children should be warned of sexual temptations and sensuous allurements (v. 3).

The consequences of an unholy union must be made perfectly clear (vv. 4–6).

We should flee temptation (v. 8).

A sexually transmitted disease may be the end product of immoral behavior (v. 11).

Sexual union should occur only in marriage (vv. 15–18).

Marital love is to be enjoyed (v. 19).

God watches all we do, including our sexual activity (v. 21).

1 CORINTHIANS 6:9–20

Habitual sexual sin may indicate a person is unsaved (vv. 9–10).

Sexual sins can be forgiven (v. 11).

Our bodies are tools for God, not for immorality (vv. 12–13).

Our bodies are important enough to be resurrected (v. 14).

We should flee, not fight, temptation (v. 18).

Sexual sin hurts us and can bring harm to our bodies (v. 18).

The Holy Spirit lives within every believer (v. 19).

God owns us (v. 19).

Jesus died to purchase us, and we should honor Him with our bodies (v. 20).

1 CORINTHIANS 7:1–9

Unmarried people have a greater freedom to serve (vv. 1, 8, 32).

Sex outside of marriage is immoral (v. 2).

The solution for passion is a spouse, not a boyfriend or a girlfriend (vv. 2, 8–9).

Married couples have free access to each other's bodies (vv. 3–4).

Men and women, husbands and wives, have strong sexual desires (vv. 3–4).

A couple's spiritual union should be more important than their physical union (v. 5).

Free access to one's spouse reduces sexual temptation (v. 5).

1 THESSALONIANS 4:1–8

Living a pure life pleases God (v. 1).

God's will is that we avoid sexual immorality (v. 3).

God wants us to learn how to control our bodies (v. 4).

Our methods of controlling our desires must be holy and honorable (v. 4).

How we control our bodies will differ from the methods of unbelievers (v. 5).

Gratifying our sexual desires outside of marriage offends and detracts from the other person (v. 6).

We should not take advantage of another person in order to satisfy our sexual desires (v. 6).

These instructions come from God, not from man (v. 8).

If we disobey these instructions, we reject God (v. 8).

NOTES

Chapter 1   Speak Now or the Wrong Person Will

1. Jane Norman and Myron W. Harris, *The Private Life of the American Teenager* (New York: Rawson, Wade, 1981), 42.
2. Cited in a letter from John McDowell to John Nieder, 4 December 1987, 1.
3. Ibid.
4. Neil Postman, *Amusing Ourselves to Death* (New York: Viking Penguin, 1985), 145–46.
5. Tipper Gore, *Raising PG Kids in an X-Rated Society* (Nashville: Abingdon, 1987), 145.
6. *Safer Sex Guidelines for Women,* distributed in the Texas House of Representatives by Rep. Ted Roberts and Rep. Bill Ceverha, 3 June 1987.
7. Mel and Norma Gabler, with James Hefley, *What Are They Teaching Our Children?* (Wheaton, IL: Victor Books, 1985), 66–67.

Chapter 2   You *Can* Teach Your Child

1. Candyce H. Stapen, "How to talk to mom and dad about sex so they won't blush," *USA Weekend,* 21–23 Nov. 1986, 16–17.
2. John Leo, "Sex and Schools," *Time,* 2 Nov. 1986, 55.

Chapter 3   The Rape of Innocence

1. David Elkind, *The Hurried Child* (Reading, MA: Addison-Wesley, 1981), 184.
2. Norman and Harris, *The Private Life,* 42–43.
3. David Elkind, *All Grown Up & No Place to Go: Teenagers in Crisis* (Reading, MA: Addison-Wesley, 1984), 3–4.
4. John LaPlace, *Health,* 3rd ed. (Englewood Cliffs, NJ: Prentice-Hall, 1980), quoted in Janet Niedhardt, "When Parents Take a Stand," *Moody Monthly,* Nov. 1982, 27.
5. Ruth Bell, et al., *Changing Bodies, Changing Lives: A Book for Teens on Sex and Relationships* (New York: Random House, 1980), 199.
6. Ibid.

Chapter 4   The Priority of Protection

1. Information gathered from A. C. Nielson, *Satellite Times,* and *TV Digest* and presented in Television Information Office, *Television Information: Winter 1987/88.*

2. TIME Charts by Cynthia Davis, in Ezra Brown, "Getting Tough," *Time*, 1 Feb. 1988, 54.

Chapter 5 The Process of Preparation

1. "Evangelical Leaders You Should Know: Profile of Dr. Bruce K. Waltke" *Moody Monthly*, July–Aug. 1987, 77–79.
2. Tim Kimmel, *Little House on the Freeway: Help for the Hurried Home* (Portland, OR: Multnomah Books, 1987), 32–33.
3. Judy Blume, *What Kids Wish They Could Tell You* (New York: Pocket Books, 1986), 10.

Chapter 6 God's Good Gift

1. Tottie Ellis, "Ads exploit people, promote promiscuity," *USA Today*, 30 Jan. 1987.

Chapter 7 The Wisdom of Waiting

1. From Ann Landers's column, newspaper and date unknown.

Chapter 8 The Path of Purity

1. Randy C. Alcorn, *Christians in the Wake of the Sexual Revolution: Recovering Our Sexual Sanity* (Portland, OR: Multnomah Press, 1985), 31.

Chapter 10 Preparation—The Early Years

1. Kenneth and Elizabeth Gangel, *Building a Christian Family* (Chicago: Moody Press, 1987), 63.
2. Grace H. Ketterman, *How to Teach Your Child about Sex* (Old Tappan, NJ: Fleming H. Revell, 1981), 33–34.

Chapter 12 Homosexuality

1. Philip Michael Ukleha, "A Theological Critique of the Contemporary Homosexual Movement," (Th.D. diss., Dallas Theological Seminary, 1982), 42–44.
2. Michael Swift, "For the Homoerotic Order, *Gay Community News*, 15 Feb. 1987, quoted in "Homosexual Threats," *Daily News Digest*, 28 Oct. 1987, 1–2.
3. William P. Wilson, "Biology, Psychology, and Homosexuality," in *What You Should Know about Homosexuality*, ed. Charles W. Foot (Grand Rapids, MI: Zondervan, 1979), 167.
4. George A. Rekers, *Growing Up Straight: What Every Family Should Know about Homosexuality* (Chicago: Moody Press, 1982), 22.
5. Ibid., 24.
6. Kenneth Gangel, *The Gospel & the Gay* (Nashville: Thomas Nelson, 1978), 41–42.

Chapter 13 AIDS and STDs

1. C. Everett Koop, quoted in David Sobel, "AIDS: What You Should Know! What You Should Tell Your Children!" *Good Housekeeping*, June 1987, 71–72.
2. Ibid., 73.
3. C. Everett Koop, *Surgeon General's Report on Acquired Immune Deficiency Syndrome* (Washington, DC: U.S. Department of Health and Human Services, 1986), 13.
4. John Seale for the House of Commons Social Services Committee, *Problems Associated with AIDS* (London: Her Majesty's Stationery Office, 13 May 1987), 144.

5. Ibid., 145.

6. Claudia Wallis, "You Haven't Heard Anything Yet," *Time*, 16 Feb. 1987, 54.

7. "The Growing Caseload," *Health Times,* Summer 1987.

8. Koop, *Surgeon General's Report,* 34.

9. Robert L. Alden, *Proverbs: A Commentary on an Ancient Book of Timeless Advice* (Grand Rapids, MI: Baker Book House, 1983), 51.

10. C. Everett Koop, "The Surgeon General Talks to *GH* Parents about AIDS Education," *Good Housekeeping,* June 1987, 74.

11. Koop, quoted in "AIDS: What You Should Know . . . ," 72.